KATHY

BOOK OF

HAPPY FAMILIES

Also by Kathy Staff

MY STORY – WRINKLES AND ALL

KATHY STAFF'S

BOOK OF

HAPPY FAMILIES

Stories, wit and wisdom
to celebrate family life

Kathy Staff
with Liz Barr

Hodder & Stoughton
LONDON SYDNEY AUCKLAND

First published in Great Britain in 1999
This paperback edition first published in 2000

The right of Kathy Staff to be identified as the Author
of the Work has been asserted by her in accordance with
the Copyright, Designs and Patents Act 1988

10 9 8 7 6 5 4 3 2 1

British Library Cataloguing in Publication Data
A record for this book is available from
the British Library

ISBN 0 340 74628 9

Printed and bound in Great Britain by
Clays Ltd, St Ives PLC

Hodder and Stoughton
A Division of Hodder Headline Ltd
338 Euston Road
London NW1 3BH

To my loving, happy family

CONTENTS

Introduction
THE RULES OF THE GAME OF
HAPPY FAMILIES

Happiness is very difficult to describe. It has no edges to it. It's much easier to tell a tragic tale – when everyone wants to know 'and what happened next?' – than to say why long periods of your life, when nothing in particular 'happened', were profoundly happy. But I do feel that one of the secrets of my own happy life has been that I have had the luck to belong to a large family.

I have always felt very blessed that I grew up in a very big family, with several generations all living in the same little Cheshire town of Dukinfield, spending time together, attending the same church, and looking out for one another. The same uncles, aunts and cousins who were around when I was young were still there when my own two daughters were born. I still have an aunt and uncle living in Dukinfield to this day, and many cousins, so our daughters, Katherine and Susan, have also grown up knowing the security and happiness that comes from being surrounded by a wide and loving family circle.

Families are like a microcosm of the whole world. If you count in all the generations of your family, and include cousins and aunts and uncles by marriage and adoption, you will probably find within your own family circle an example of almost every sort of person. Every family has its eccentric ones, its clever ones, its beautiful ones, its unhappy ones, its lazy ones, its successes and failures, its rogues and its saints. Just because you are all related to one another doesn't mean that you will all be alike. What it *does* mean is that you can all be there for one another. It's the best place to learn how to get on with the whole world.

Once you've got a loving family background you can spread the love through other families. In my young day the neighbours in the street where you lived were an extension of your family. They were your friends and companions, and looked out for you. I even had an Uncle Fred and Auntie Alice who treated their budgie as a member of our extended family. You would often see them out in the car on a Saturday or Sunday afternoon, and Auntie Alice would have the budgie, in a cage, on her knee – taking it out for a trip in the car! It was a wonderful sight: Auntie Alice, sitting in the front with the budgie in its cage on her knee, saying to it, 'We're just taking you out for a run in the country!'

I've heard people say that family life as we know it will become a thing of the past when the new millennium begins. With an increasing divorce rate, people moving away from old familiar neighbourhoods, and with both parents going out to work, many children have little experience of growing up in traditional families. In times of crisis, professional counsellors are replacing the extended family support system provided by brothers and sisters, aunts, uncles and grandparents. People are forgetting how to make family life work for them. I'm sure I am not alone in thinking that this is a terrible shame.

The world has changed a great deal since I was a young mother bringing up my family, and even more so since I was a child. Of course, I realise now that that was a golden age when, if you were ill, you knocked on the wall to your neighbour, who went to find your *family* doctor – who usually lived a few doors away and who would call at your home day or night.

Pressures have increased on us all since then, not only on the poor overworked doctors. We don't live in stable, permanent communities. People have to move to find work. Both parents have to work long hours to keep a home together, and children come home from school to an empty house. Will family life survive all these changes into the next millennium? I believe it has *got* to, or it could be the end of the world. I firmly believe that this is what we are brought into the world to do: to love one another. If people stop loving their families, they will stop loving anybody.

'Family' needn't only mean our blood relations, or relations through marriage. Close friends can become your family. Even friendly neighbours and workmates can become 'family'. Your favourite hobby or club can provide you with the sort of friendship and support that an extended family gives. Above all, if you belong to a church, you are immediately a member of the Christian family. However your family is made up, there have always been unwritten rules about how to make it work. You have to learn to share treasured possessions and your time.

There has to be give and take. Above all, there has to be love.

So that is why I felt I wanted to write this little book.

I want to talk about all those unwritten rules that used to make for happy family life in the old days, and which I believe still can. I've remembered many of the things my mother used to say. It sounds like a joke, doesn't it? 'As my dear old mother used to say ... ' But if you had a loving mother, you do think back on how she did things, and what she taught you. So 'things that my mother taught me' will quite often crop up in what follows.

I wasn't sure how to begin this book. Then I started thinking about the card game of 'Happy Families' that we used to play when our children were little. I found an old pack and read the instructions, and it seems to me that they could start us off. Just to remind you, here are the rules of the game:

Happy Families – a game for any number of people – although there must be at least three

1 The **Families** are: Bun the Baker; his wife, Mrs Bun; his son, Master Bun; and his daughter, Miss Bun ...

   And there are also the families of Grits the Grocer, Bones the Butcher, Dose the Doctor, Block the Barber, Pots the Painter, Bung the Brewer, Tape the Tailor, Chip the Carpenter, Soot the Sweep and Dip the Dyer.

2 Each **Player** contributes counters to a **Counters Pool**, placed together on the table.

3 The **Character Cards** are shuffled and cut,

4 and dealt by the **Dealer**.

5 The Players take up their cards and look at them.

6 The player to the left of the Dealer is the first to **Play the Game**. He must decide which cards he needs in his hand to make up a whole Family. He can ask any other Player for any Character Card he needs to make up a Family. (A Player cannot ask for a Character Card unless he holds at least one member of that Family in his hand.)

7 The Player who has been asked must produce the card asked for if he has it. If, however, he has not got this particular card he replies, '**Not at Home**', and then it is his turn. A Player who is successful in getting the card he asks for continues to ask other Players for other cards he needs until he receives the reply, 'Not at Home'.

   As Families are completed they are placed face down on the table in front of the Players who completed them.

8 **The Optional 'Please' and 'Thank You' Rule**: If you operate this rule, each Player, when asking for a card, *must* say '**Please** may I have … Mrs Bun?' If he forgets to say 'Please', he loses his turn to the Player he has asked. And when a card is handed over he *must* say, '**Thank You**'. If he forgets, the Player who handed the card over takes it back, but he too must remember to say 'Please' and 'Thank you' or he too loses his turn.

9 The **Winner** is the Player with the most completed Families in front of him when everyone has finished their turn, and he wins all the counters from the pool.

In this book, the rules go like this:

1 **The Happy Family**: The butchers, bakers and candlestick-makers of Dukinfield.

2 **The Counters Pool**: Differences in family fortunes.

3 **The Character Cards**: Pantomime and Bible heroes and heroines.

4 **The Dealer**: Blessings and sorrows of family life.

5 **The Players (any number over three)**: The extended family.

6 **Playing the Game**: The family that plays together stays together.

7 **'Not at Home'**: The decline of the old neighbourhood communities.

8 **The Optional 'Please' and 'Thank You' Rule**: Family life as portrayed by TV soaps and dramas.

9 **The Winner**: The family that prays together stays together.

Endgame

I hope everybody will want to play my kind of 'Happy Families', and help to preserve the traditions of family life into the new millennium. I have even ended each chapter with six strategies to help you win the game!

1
THE HAPPY FAMILY

My own family tree consists of people with names and occupations rather like Mr Bun the Baker and Mr Grits the Grocer of the Happy Families card game!

Meet the Higginbottoms and the Hartleys – the butchers, the bakers and candlestick-makers of Dukinfield

If you haven't read my autobiography, you won't know that I was christened Minnie. My mother had really wanted to name me Leonora, after her favourite brother Leonard, my uncle, who was killed at the very end of the First World War. But everyone said to her, 'Ah! Don't call her that ... everyone will call her Nora!' (On my Girl Guide's honour, this is true.) So, in order to be a good mother and protect her daughter from such a terrible fate, she chose another name – Minnie – instead. (I'm not sure if there are many baptisms these days of 'Minnies'!) My sister was christened Constance, and so all through our childhood we were the terrible two, Connie and Minnie Higginbottom.

I changed my name when I was twenty-one to Katherine Brant because I didn't feel Minnie Higginbottom was quite right, somehow, for an aspiring actress, which is what I was. Nowadays you would probably go quite far with a name like Minnie Higginbottom – but not in those days. Well, I didn't think so anyway, and I'd always wanted to be called Katherine. And then a year or two later I married John Staff, so I have been Kathy Staff ever since.

The family tree

We were never alone when we were small. Most of my family lived in Dukinfield; aunts and uncles lived all around us. If you needed any help, you turned to your family, and they were there.

Uncle Clement (Clem) married Doris, my favourite auntie, on 4 September 1939, the day after war broke out, and we had planned to hold the wedding reception at the church school. However, we had no materials for 'blacking out' the windows. Con and I had to carry all the food across to the only place in Dukinfield that had got proper blackout curtains, which was the Lime Street Working Men's Club – which none of us had ever entered before, all being strictly teetotal.

Most of my mother's side of the family practised abstinence. Grandpa and Grandma Hartley met because they were both secretaries of their different Temperance Societies. My mother and father both signed the pledge and gave lantern lectures at the Mission on the evils of drink when they were first married. I signed the pledge when I was a teenager, and I have never had a glass of alcohol in my life.

Grandma and Grandpa Higginbottom were not so strict. They did like a glass of wine with their food, and that side of the family still does. (I think that's where my sister Connie and daughter Katherine must get it from!) Grandpa Higginbottom used to like stout, and Grandma used to put a hot poker in it to make it go all frothy.

There were many Hartleys and Higginbottoms in my parents' generation – and they all lived and worked in or around Dukinfield. They had shops in Astley Steet and King Street. My father's father was a boilermaker. Grandpa Hartley had a hardware business, with a shop on the corner of Robert Street. Uncle Clem was a butcher. Uncle Sam was a baker with a confectionery shop. Uncle Harry, who is still going strong, worked at the Co-op in the grocery department. They sound just like people off the Happy Families playing cards, don't they? Butcher or baker or candlestick-maker, they were all staunch Christians and all attended St Mark's Church, Dukinfield.

So we were a large clan – one big happy family. At one time we had sixteen members of the family all in the church choir.

Every Sunday night after church, all the Hartley side of the family used to go round to Grandma Hartley's. My sister Con and I used to go to Grandma Higginbottom's after Sunday School, then we used to go on home for Sunday lunch, because Mother always cooked a proper Sunday lunch, but after the service on Sunday nights we all used to gather at Grandma Hartley's house behind the family hardware shop. We met to talk and eat, and of course to have a sing-song round the piano. It sounds like something out of the history books now, but that's how it was.

Turning off the television and having fun

Child neglect has always been a problem – parents who don't have enough time to spend with their children, or simply don't want to spend time with their children. Or the only time they do spend with them, they are telling them off, or taking them to school, or down to the shops, but only to buy boring things like household goods. You hear them sometimes, shouting at their children in the supermarkets. Not really caring for them or enjoying their company, or helping them develop as people.

I've no personal experience of this, but you do hear that some people come home from work, and just fling money at the kids saying, 'Go to the fish and chip shop and get yourself something to eat.' I suppose you can understand that if the mother has been working hard all day she doesn't feel up to cooking her children a nice meal, but it can't lead to a very happy family life.

I think it is so important for parents to spend as much time as they can with their children. We should all spend time together as a family, sharing meals, going on outings, doing things for fun, and *not* leaving all that side of life up to the BBC, ITV and SKY. Even if you are too busy at work during the day to spend much time with your children, the very best way to end their day when they are little is to tuck them up and read them a bedtime story.

The extended family support group

I'm sure the wider family support in the old days helped hold marriages together. A young married couple would rent a house as near as possible to the wife's parents' home, and it was the love and support of the whole family that helped the newlyweds through the difficult early years. Then, as now, it was often a struggle for a young couple to make ends meet, and they were inexperienced in dealing with many of life's problems.

But these days many seem to want their own place, go their own way, and move as far away from parents and in-laws as possible. I do think this is such a mistake. I know it can't always be avoided, because people have to move for their jobs, but it looks to me as though many people are deliberately choosing to keep away from their families.

I think people have forgotten how to make a commitment, or don't realise that you sometimes need help to stick to it. Marriage should be for life, but after the first big quarrel so many couples just 'throw in the towel'. When they don't have the support of the family to turn to – when it's just the two of them, always alone together, perhaps with not much money and living in a small flat – no wonder they find it easier to run away from their problems than to see them through.

When John and I were married, he automatically became a member of my family, and soon became, as he still is, a very active member of our church family. I always remember my mother exclaiming, 'Well! I never thought the day would come when I would be talked about in St Mark's as "John Staff's mother-in-law"!'

Family treats

My Uncle Peter worked as a commercial traveller – as they called them in those days – and after the war he got a job with a toy firm in Salford. How my two girls used to love it when he was in the area, because he always called in at my mum's and had lunch. His van was full of toys and, if we were there, he would give them a little something out of the back.

Auntie Alice is the aunt who is still with us, aged ninety-one. She married Tom Gregson, who we all thought was 'a cut above', because he worked in an office, being treasurer at the Mill. He always used to say to Con and me whenever we went to see them, 'Oh dear! If only I had known you were coming I'd have made you some chips. Now *next* time you come there will be chips.' But we never got chips. It was always going to be the great treat *next* time, but every time we got there it was, 'Well, what a shame – if I'd only known …' We were never given chips, not once.

My Uncle Fred was wonderful with our children. He had a 'money tree', with sixpenny bits 'growing' on it. Every time we went round to see him and Auntie Alice (the auntie with the budgie that used to go out with her in the car) there was always some money under the rug from this money tree. 'Just look what fell out of the money tree this morning … It must have known you were coming!'

When we were young they moved away for a time, to near Doncaster, and they had a sweet shop. Fred used to send us 'mouldy' chocolate. It had to be 'mouldy' chocolate, or my mother would insist on sending him the money for it. Of course, it wasn't mouldy at all. He would send us a parcel every so often and he always wrote, 'This is some mouldy chocolate! I thought I'd send it to you because I couldn't sell it in the shop.'

Fred went on being a wonderful uncle to my children when they came along. They never wanted for anything if he knew about it.

Sharing your good fortune

We never had much money when I was a child, but my mother had a few premium bonds and once or twice her numbers came up. It would never have occurred to her to keep the money for herself. She always shared her win with all the family. And that's what we have always done in our family. If anyone has some good fortune, we share it.

Uncle Sam and Auntie Alice had a confectioner's shop just up the road from my secondary school so I used to go to them for lunch every day. When I left school they wanted me to 'go into' the shop with them. They also wanted to leave me the business, because they had no children. In those days working in a bakery meant getting up at four in the morning to light the fire, and I'm afraid I said, 'No thank you very much!' But they were very kind. They gave Con spending money when she was at university, and they paid towards my singing and piano lessons.

Working together in adversity

The day my father died, aged sixty-two, he didn't even gasp, his head just fell back and he died. I was sitting on the chair beside him, and we had just had a cup of tea. He loved his cup of tea. My two girls were playing on the floor, and my mother was sitting in her usual place by the fire. When we suddenly realised something was wrong, I ran up the street to get help, because my mother didn't have a telephone. Uncle Clem's wife, Doris, had a sister, Mary, who had a shop just a little way up Astley Street. I ran in and asked her to telephone the doctor for us. Then I ran back to my mother. Mary must have telephoned Uncle Clem as well, because even before the doctor got there, Clem had arrived. He took one look at my dad, and then picked him up off the chair just as though he were a baby and carried him through and put him on the bed.

The doctor said there was nothing we could have done to save him. It was just his time. He was called, and he went. He had just had a cup of tea, and he always loved his cup of tea. A sad moment that none of us there will ever forget in our whole lives.

The last of the Higginbottoms

Uncle Harry is the last of the Higginbottoms. It's strange, with all that family of six, only two had children. My father had two daughters, Connie and me, and first of all I changed my name to Brant, and then we both married, so neither of us kept the name going. Auntie Alice also had two daughters, Ruth and Anne, who have also both married, but in any case their family name is Gregson.

So Uncle Harry is the last one with the proud old name of Higginbottom. At eighty-five he still goes to church every Sunday. He has had to leave the choir because he can't see clearly enough to read the music, but he still attends and sits in the family pew. At one time in the Church of England people used to pay to have a reserved family pew. All our pews at St Mark's have always been free, but families always sat together in a regular pew that they regarded as 'their pew'. When I was young, there used to be times, especially at Easter and Christmas, when you couldn't be sure of getting a seat. We used to say, 'We'd better get there early or else we shan't get our pew.' But nowadays we have no problem, unfortunately. I think it would be lovely to arrive and find some new members of the church family sitting there.

Katherine and Susan have a strong sense of belonging to a large clan. They grew up with two sets of grandparents living nearby, and all my cousins, to whom I am very close, and who have all had children and grandchildren. Many of them still live in and around Dukinfield, so we're still a big family. Katherine, John and I all attend St Mark's and sing in the choir. Every time we go to church we see my cousin, Frances, and her children and grandchildren, and one of her grandsons, Richard, is a server, so yet another generation is taking over.

Unfortunately, I don't think now that John and I will ever be grandparents. That's a big disappointment, but it seems to be the way God has decided it should be. Many people in Britain nowadays don't have children or, like us, don't have grandchildren. It can happen for all sorts of reasons. It is a shared sadness for many people and is all the more reason why it is important to build up supportive relationships with your neighbours and friends, to create a wide 'extended' family network.

I think we are supposed to love and encourage the succeeding generations of children, even when they are not our own flesh and blood. Children with busy parents often love to discover a friendly 'granny' neighbour to talk to, even if she's not really their granny. Coming together in shared moments is what family life is all about. Working together in adversity, laughing together when there is good news, binds people together, and even a stranger becomes 'family'.

STRATEGIES FOR HAPPY FAMILIES

* Research your own family tree and all its branches.

* Get in touch with everybody on it.

* The family that prays together stays together.

* Let your marriage partner become a member of your family.

* Build up a 'family' support group with friends and neighbours.

* Stand together in times of adversity.

'... And in thee shall all families of the earth be blessed' (*Genesis 12:3, AV*).

2
THE COUNTERS POOL

Before the game of Happy Families begins, the rules say that each Player must put three counters into a pool. It made me think of the parable of the talents, where one servant was given five talents, another two, and another one. When their Lord and master returned, he wanted to know what they had each done with the talents he had given them. The only one he was angry with was the one who had done nothing – just buried his talent in the ground to hide it. He hadn't even had the fun of playing Happy Families with it!

So what talents have you and I been given to put in the Counters Pool?

My mother's contribution to my first autograph book

Be good sweet maid, and let who will be clever
Do noble deeds, don't dream them all day long
And so make life, death and that vast forever
One glad, sweet song.

Where do you come from?

My roots are from typical north of England working-class stock. I was born into a family of 'salt of the earth' sort of people, with their heads 'screwed on', who all worked hard in the mills, in the iron foundries, or were salesmen or shopkeepers. They were not in the least pretentious, but I suppose they had some 'middle-class aspirations'. They certainly wanted their children to have every possible opportunity to better themselves.

When I was a child no one branch of the family was any better off than any other, with the possible exception of Auntie Alice, who married Tom Gregson, who worked in an office, so he was the one that we always thought was 'a cut above'. They bought a brand-new house when they were first married – and she is still living in it, aged ninety-one. It must have been his money they bought it with, because it certainly couldn't have been Alice's – she didn't have any. But she did sort of 'better' herself by marrying Tom. I've got a solid-silver napkin ring that Auntie Alice gave me, although I never use it now – because it's engraved with the initials M. H. for Minnie Higginbottom.

First find your rainbow

Within any family, different members will have different things they are good at. One may be clever, another beautiful, another may have a beautiful singing voice. My sister Connie was pretty, with naturally wavy hair; and she was also intelligent, quiet and hard working. (She still is all those things!) I was never pretty, my hair hung straight as a die, I was not particularly clever, and I always did as little school work as I could get away with before running outside to climb trees or swing round the lamp-post.

They always said I should have been a 'Peter' really. I was very like my Uncle Peter, and always up to something, while Connie sat neat and quiet in the corner with her book. I got mucky and dirty, and of course we didn't have hot water on tap like now. It was a lot more work to clean me up.

I used to think that Connie had been given all the family talents, and there wasn't anything left for me. But when I was cast as a fairy in the church pantomime one Christmas, I knew what my path in life had to be. I had set my heart on going on the stage as a ballet dancer – and from that moment I didn't mind about any of the rest. As I was only three at the time, you can see I didn't have too long to wait before I discovered my own ambitions and dreams.

Family life has responsibilities that sometimes mean not fulfilling your own dreams

My mother left school when she was eleven. She won a scholarship to the grammar school but just at that time her younger sister, Ada, was born. My mother had to stay at home to help her own mother, who was stone deaf, to look after the baby, as well as running the hardware shop. You did in those days.

My mother was very clever, and going to grammar school would have been wonderful for her. She might even have developed her talent as a singer, because she had a beautiful singing voice that was never trained. But then, if she *had* gone to grammar school she might have gone on to university, and then she probably wouldn't have married my father – because *she* would have become 'a cut above'. So I would not be here now to tell you about her.

God is working his purpose out

Something else happened to change my mother's destiny. I've mentioned her brother, my Uncle Leonard, who was a volunteer killed in the First World War. He was going to become a priest when the war was over, and everyone thought that he would be the first member of our family to be ordained, so they were very proud of him. He was planning to live and work abroad as a missionary. My mother trained to be a nurse, and Con and I have always thought that if Uncle Leonard had not been killed, she would have gone with him to Africa and worked alongside him. She was very devout, and very close to Leonard, and we are sure that that was her original idea.

It was terrible when he died. He was firing a gun, and two shells met in the middle, and his own shell came back as a ricochet and killed him. It happened just days before the First World War ended. That was the really sad thing. Leonard was a key person in my mother's life, and what happened to him altered everything. She was a very long time getting over it. But once again, if she had gone to Africa with him, she wouldn't have married my dad, and I wouldn't be here telling you the story.

My mother would be so happy and proud to know that it is her own youngest granddaughter, Susan, who has now become the first member of the family to be ordained a priest in the Church of England. I don't know whether Susan has ever thought seriously about missionary work abroad. I think God's Church in Africa probably needs to send their missionaries over to Britain these days, to convert the heathen over here. My mother never lost her own devout faith, but it must have sometimes been hard for her to know how God would work his purpose out, when her own hopes and dreams seemed to have been so often thwarted.

The best laid plans of mice and men ...

My father's life, too, was turned upside down by the events of war. Until the Second World War started he had been doing rather well, working his way up the ladder until he was the assistant manager of a Bradford company, the Provident Clothing and Supply Company, running their Ashton office. He was forty when he got his call-up papers and joined the Royal Artillery as a driver.

He was too old for the life. Five years later he ended up driving all the way through France into Germany as part of the Allied Front pushing the Germans back. He had to sleep in the open air, under his vehicle. At his age, and with a weak chest from working in his youth in the Manchester cotton mills, it was too much for him. He got a cerebral thrombosis one hot day while swimming in a river in Germany. A German boy saw he was in trouble, dived in, and saved his life.

When he came home he was a complete invalid, and suffered from painful fits and attacks for the rest of his life.

The doctors said he would never work again. He took life quite gently. He had a little seat half-way down the garden, and I can see him now, sitting there just surveying it all. He loved his garden, and spent a lot of time there.

However, he said he couldn't just sit around doing nothing, and he managed to find work in a big rope-works in Dukinfield, where he could sit and unwind the twine. It wasn't what he'd been used to, though. Then a job came up in the storerooms, so he was moved there as storeman. There were no windows, and the delivery trap door to the mill was high up at the top. Whenever the side was opened for a delivery to be hoisted up, Dad would stand by the opening, gazing across to the hills. He used to love that, and used to stand right on the edge. He'd say, 'It was beautiful today – looking across at the hills …' And my mother used to get a bit het up about it, and would say, 'Well, you shouldn't be standing on the edge like that! You could fall!'

Connie and Minnie – Girl Guides

When we were young our church started a Girl Guide group. Originally we were all in the Girls' Brigade. I loved the Girls' Brigade because we had a nice band. We used to do marching. A girl called Dora Facer played the big drum, and other people played various instruments. I used to enjoy marching up and down. I just marched about – I didn't play an instrument. We didn't learn anything as such; it was all just good fun. So of course a lot of them, like Con, who was always very keen to learn, decided to change to the more educational Girl Guide Association.

We all had to vote. Aged ten and a half, I was the only one who voted *not* to change to the Girl Guides. But everyone else was for it, so that was the end of the Girls' Brigade and the beginning of the Guides Association at our church.

I did join the Guides – because everyone else did. Con became a Patrol Leader, of course– that was natural. But in the end even I got quite a few badges. I actually enjoyed myself, because I learned how to tie all sorts of different knots. We did lots of different things – like tracking. A crowd of us would set out for a walk, and we'd leave tracking signs, so that the next group could follow. But when we went on rambles I always used to ask, 'Is it on a bus route?' so that if I got tired, I knew I could come back on the bus. That was the kind of Guide I was. I was a tomboy and liked climbing trees, but I didn't like going for long walks. Guides seemed to walk for miles.

We were taught how to light a campfire and cook on it, but Con and I went camping only once. I didn't really take to camping, I'm afraid. I didn't like the native life. I remember one night we were asleep in the tent, and I woke up to find a great big beetle on my pillow. I woke Con, screaming, 'There's a beetle!' She sat up, got out her Guide knife, cut the beetle in two, and threw it out of the tent. I was appalled, and that was the end of camping for me. I didn't want to commune with nature so close at hand.

One day the Chief Guide came to Ashton, and everybody turned out to meet her. Our Con was chosen to carry the Chief Guide's Standard – which was the greatest honour any Guide could wish for. I was in the choir, standing at the back. My dad said afterwards, 'I could tell which one was you, because of the wavy brim of your hat!' We used to wear big Girl Guide hats, and I'd sat on mine. However hard my mother tried to make me look smart, it never worked. My hat brim was always wavy. And there was my sister, absolutely immaculate, carrying the Standard, and there was I, standing at the back with my wavy hat. And my dad saying, 'Well, at least I could tell which one was you ...'

Accept your family as they are – and love them anyway

My sister Con went to grammar school, but I did not pass my eleven-plus. On the day I was sitting it – it was a Saturday – Auntie Doris, Clem's wife, arrived at our house with two tickets for the ballet. I definitely wanted to go to the ballet instead of sitting my exam, and I said so.

My mother said, 'You will go and sit your exam.'

I said, 'I want to go to the ballet.'

I had to go and sit the exam of course, but I was so disappointed and annoyed about missing the ballet that I just sat in the exam room, and more or less gave up. As I've said, I didn't pass. I have never taken any other examination, not even an acting examination, since that day. I still think I should have gone to see the ballet! I have always loved it, and still do.

My sister Connie went to university, and became a teacher. She was Head of English at Wakefield High and then she was Deputy Head of her school in Sheffield until her retirement a few years ago.

I went to Lakes Road Secondary Modern, and became

School Captain, and my headmistress, Miss Wood, said that I had the capability to run an office – the only trouble being that she didn't think anyone would ever let me! After I left school at fourteen – without taking a single examination of course – I became a reasonably proficient shorthand typist. We were all trained for something, because my mother, even more than my father, didn't want us to miss out on any opportunities. A year later I joined the National Gas and Oil Engine Company Limited (not the National Theatre, more is the pity!) In the normal run of things it would have been me who would still be working class in our family. With my poor education, my expectations were low. If I hadn't turned to the theatre, I doubt I would have risen very far.

Both my parents were happy for us as we were. There was no pressure. They didn't love me any less than Connie even though I was all over the place, while she was good and studious and successful. They helped me to make my own choices and to do the things I wanted to do. I wasn't brainy or brilliant like Con, but our mum and dad loved us both just the same. They appreciated that we were both completely different. I don't think they worried about me at all. They thought I would make a very good secretary and would be more than happy doing that.

From my autograph book

> 'When you're up to your neck in hot water – just think of the kettle, and sing!'

A girl called Joyce Gerish wrote that. I always remember her. We were both Head Girls together at Lakes Road, and then we both went to the National and got jobs there. As she was a very tall, good-looking girl with blonde hair, how they ever came to choose me as well, I shall never know.

'Many that are first shall be last; and the last first' (Mark 10:31)

I *was* good at being a secretary. I sometimes think I knew more about shorthand typing and organising an office than I do now about acting. I only act from my feeling inside. I've never been trained – never went to drama school. But while I worked by day in an office, I spent all my free time acting in amateur productions. At one time I was acting in five different productions at the same time; I was out every night of the week, and my mother said I was using home like a hotel. Eventually I took a deep breath and applied for a job as student-actress for a touring repertory company that I had seen advertised in *The Stage*. I got the job, and I have never looked back.

I was thrown in at the deep end with that company. They were touring little villages in Scotland, and we had to learn and perform a new play every night. It certainly taught you how to learn lines quickly. When I moved on to a more regular repertory company, doing a new play every week instead of every night, it seemed like a great luxury.

Hardly anyone went to drama school when I was young. Every town had a repertory theatre, and those interested went into that. We all learned by *doing* it. I still don't know any 'method' or way of doing things. I only know how I feel and how I see the character as I read the part. If you do something with all your heart, because you love doing it, I think that you are bound to become quite good at it.

I remember when I was playing Mrs Watty in *The Corn is Green* at Oldham Rep. A new girl was meant to be playing Bessie Watty, but for some reason Carl Paulsen, the administrator, didn't think she was right, and suddenly announced to the company that she'd left. At that time Anne Kirkbride, Deirdre from *Coronation Street*, was our Assistant Stage Manager. I can see her now, as he was speaking, squatting down on the floor, painting some props. Carl said, 'And Anne is going to play Bessie Watty.' Anne's face! I'll never forget it. She'd never acted on a professional stage before, but she worked hard, and she never went back to painting scenery. She went into *Coronation Street* after Oldham Rep and has been a household name ever since.

That was how people used to get on. You got paid hardly anything, but if you were prepared to work hard you could get on.

I had a few very happy years in repertory theatre, and then when I was twenty-two I met, and a year later married, John Staff. We didn't have any money, so we moved into a house with his parents, and shared it with them. I gave up the theatre and returned to office work, because I could earn more money that way. John's salary in the Air Force during his National Service, and then as a teacher afterwards, didn't amount to much at first, and I could earn more in an office than on the stage. We wanted to save up to buy our own house as soon as possible. (It's one thing to live *near* your in-laws, quite another to share a house with them!) I missed the theatre, but I wasn't unhappy – I had always intended to stop work for a few years anyway when we started a family. I always wanted to be at home and bring up my own babies.

Count your blessings

The happiest days of my life were probably when the children were young. We had our own lovely home in Dukinfield, my father and mother were living nearby, I was married to John, who was teaching at the grammar school and – the icing on the cake – I could return to acting. When the children were old enough I discovered that I could work during the day for Granada Television in Manchester, and still be at home in time to put them to bed. I started taking 'walk on' parts – in new series like *Coronation Street*!

At first I was only doing odd bits and pieces, working for just two or three days a month. I never visualised myself as a star; I was a jobbing actress. Whatever part it was, I just loved doing it. I never thought about fame or fortune; I simply wanted to act. It was a very happy time. And if I hadn't got on, I think I would still have been perfectly happy. I was never very ambitious.

I was happy then, and I am happy now, with the way things have turned out. I'm happy with my lot. I've been fortunate, God has been good to me, and I am very contented.

Some people, however fortunate they are, seem never to be contented. Some people, however unfortunate, are always happy. It's a matter of temperament I suppose.

You never can tell

When our daughters were young, it was Katherine who was the more out-going one, the one always wanting to be off and away playing with her friends. I used to say to her,

'Now wait for Susan. Take her with you.' But Susan used to say, 'I don't want to go.' So Katherine was out and about while Susan played quietly in her room at home.

But when they grew older, Katherine didn't leave home even when she went to teachers' training college. I thought it would be better if she went right away, and got herself immersed in student life, but she chose to go to Manchester, which was just a half-an-hour bus ride away. And she has lived and worked in this area ever since.

Susan was always the quiet one, so when she suddenly announced that she had applied for a job working in London, you could have knocked us down with a feather. She loved it. She still loves London. Katherine doesn't. She won't ever come to London with us. She has stayed here in Cheshire, while Susan has gone zooming off.

They are both very independently minded girls, and have made good lives and careers for themselves. But while Susan seems to be on a journey, and keeps moving on, step by step, Katherine seems to be quite settled. She has stayed in the same job, in dentistry, for nearly twenty years now, and has made her home in the same familiar neighbourhood, surrounded by family and friends. It just goes to show, you never can tell.

STRATEGIES FOR THE COUNTERS POOL

* Don't make fun of your ugly ducklings – help them to turn into swans.

* Discover your dreams.

* Don't always put your own ambitions first – someone else's need may be greater than yours.

* Be happy with your lot, and count your blessings.

* Love all your children equally, even the naughty ones, and don't make them feel they must compete.

* Have faith in the future – even when things don't seem to be turning out the way you hope.

'To every thing there is a season, and a time to every purpose under the heaven' (*Ecclesiastes 3:1, AV*)

3
THE CHARACTER CARDS

The personalities painted on the cards in a game of Happy Families are comic and grotesque, rather like pantomime characters. I'm sure Mrs Bun would make an excellent Dame, while Master Dose the Doctor's son reminds me of all those Silly Billies, Simple Simons and Wishee Washees that a pantomime Dame always has as her useless assistant. Mrs Block the Barber's wife would make an elegant Fairy Godmother, and in some productions she might even make it to Principal Girl! I think I would cast Miss Grits the Grocer's daughter as Principal Boy. Mr Dip the Dyer could be the Demon King and Mr Tape the Tailor looks as though he is a natural for Baron Hard Up!

Like the game of Happy Families, pantomimes are stories with a very good moral for life, and they can help with character building. Some of them even remind me of stories in the Bible.

Sunday school stories

The girl who runs the Sunday School at St Mark's told us at the last parish meeting that when the service and Sunday School both started at ten o'clock, many more children came. But now our service has been moved back to nine-thirty, fewer parents are bringing their children. They used to drop them off at Sunday School at ten o'clock and then go home to read the Sunday papers in peace or go and do some shopping. But since the shops aren't open at nine-thirty, or perhaps because they need their lie-in bed on a Sunday morning, they are no longer bringing their children to the Sunday School as much as they used to.

I used to think it was so sad that people would use a church just to leave their children somewhere so that they could have some peace and quiet on a Sunday morning, rather than coming to church together as a family. But now the children aren't even getting the chance to come to Sunday School, which these days is a lot of fun as well as instructive. My two daughters really loved it when they went, and got up to all sorts of things. It was much stricter in my day.

When I was a child we used to go to Sunday School every week. We had a very big Sunday School, and one thing we always had to do was to learn the Collect, the short prayer written for that week, and know it by heart:

Collect for the twenty-first Sunday after Trinity:

Grant, we beseech Thee, merciful Lord,
To Thy faithful people pardon and peace,
That they may be cleansed from all their sins
And serve Thee with a quiet mind;
Through Jesus Christ, our Lord, Amen.

Book of Common Prayer

At ten-thirty, when we'd finished at Sunday School, we joined our parents at the service in church; then we had Sunday School again in the afternoon and another church service in the evening.

My grandmother was very strict, and even when you were at home on a Sunday you weren't allowed to play with your toys. You could read a book or write a letter. My mother was the same, just as strict. Occasionally as a child I used to feel, 'Oh dear. Do I have to go again?' But it did me no harm, and once I was there, I did enjoy myself, especially when we had stories read to us from the Bible, and then discussed the stories.

The 'best-seller' that is seldom read

The Bible is the best-selling book in the world, and yet I think it is read the least. People buy it, but then they don't seem to realise how good the stories are. It seems such a pity that so many people put their Bible in the bookcase, thinking, 'I know I ought to read it, but it's boring.' I remember the first time the story of David and Goliath was read to me in Sunday School, from the Book of Samuel in the Old Testament. I thought it was the most exciting story I'd ever heard:

THE STORY OF DAVID AND GOLIATH

There on the mountainside stood the mighty Philistine army, standing against the army of King Saul and the children of Israel. The opposing camps were pitched on the slopes of two mountains, with a great valley in between. The Philistines sent out their champion, Goliath of Gath, a giant of a man who wore armour of bronze and wielded an enormous iron spear as big as a tree. Goliath called across the valley and challenged King Saul to choose a champion from his own army to fight him man to man and the winner would take all. King Saul and the men of Israel were very afraid, because none of them felt strong enough to fight such a giant.

And out steps a young shepherd boy, David, who has been sent to visit the battlefield by his father with some food for his older brothers, all conscripts in Saul's army.

David was very interested when he arrived at the army camp to discover everyone talking about Goliath and discussing who could possibly be brave and strong enough to accept his challenge. David said to his older brothers, 'Who is this uncircumcised Philistine, that he should defy the armies of the living God?' And his brothers were cross with him and his oldest brother said, 'What are you doing here? You are very naughty to have left your sheep. You just wanted an excuse to come and see the battle.' (A typical older brother's remark!)

And David, like any child, said, 'What have I done now? I'm just saying – why does nobody do anything about this Philistine?'

Someone told King Saul that there was a young shepherd boy going round the camp asking why nobody wanted to accept Goliath's challenge. So the king sent for him, and David said to Saul, 'Let no man's heart fail because of this great giant. I will kill him for you.'

When Saul laughed and told him he couldn't possibly fight Goliath, because he was too young and inexperienced, David (rather boastfully) told the king that he had already killed a lion and a bear when looking after his father's sheep. Then he said, 'God delivered me from the paw of the lion and the paw of the bear. He will certainly keep me safe from this Philistine.'

And so it was agreed that David would be the champion for the army of Israel. Saul insisted that David wear his own royal armour and his own personal sword, a very great honour. But when David put it on, he couldn't move in it, because it was far too big and heavy for him. So he took it all off again, and went out into the valley to face Goliath armed only with his shepherd's staff, a sling (what we might call a catapult today), and five smooth stones which he picked up out of a stream and put into his shepherd's bag.

Goliath, in his heavy brass armour, with a shield-bearer carrying his shield in front of him, looked across the valley at young David with utter disgust and disdain. He felt insulted that they had sent a young boy with a stick to meet his mighty challenge, 'Am I a dog?' he said 'that you come at me with staves?' And he cursed David. But David stood his

35

ground and called back, 'You come to me with a sword and spear and shield, but I come to you in the name of the Lord of hosts, the God of Israel, whom you have defied. This day will the Lord deliver you into my hand, and I will kill you, and I will cut off your head that all the earth may know that there is a God in Israel. And everyone shall know that the Lord saves not with sword and spear, for the battle is the Lord's.'

Then, as the great Philistine warrior advanced on him, the young shepherd boy ran forward, took out a stone from his bag, and put it in his sling. He must have done it many times when wolves were attacking his sheep.

He flung the stone, hitting Goliath right in the middle of his forehead, and this gigantic man fell down stone dead. Then David took the Philistine giant's own sword, and cut off his head. And all the Philistines fled in terror.

Was that boring? Now be honest.

Pantomime heroes and heroines

People happily go every year with their children to watch a pantomime, but I have noticed that many pantomime stories have direct parallels with Bible stories.

In *Jack and the Beanstalk* for example, the principal character is a young boy, very poor and rather naughty, who rids the world of a wicked giant who has been making terrible threats: 'Fee! Fie! Foe! Fum! I smell the blood of an Englishman. Be he alive or be he dead, I'll grind his bones to bake my bread!'

Aided no doubt by Mrs Bun (playing Jack's mother) and against all the odds, Jack cleverly kills the giant by getting him to charge after him down his beanstalk, and then cutting it down when the giant is still at the top. He changes from being a naughty, cheeky boy into a great hero. Just like the story of David and Goliath.

Sleeping Beauty ends like the story in the New Testament of Jesus raising Jairus' daughter. Do you remember? A desperately worried father comes to find Jesus and asks him for his help because his daughter is on the brink of death. Then a message comes to say that it is already too late, the little girl has died. Everyone thinks she is dead, but just like the handsome prince in the pantomime who kisses the Sleeping Beauty awake from her long sleep, Jesus says, 'She is not dead. She is only asleep.' He doesn't kiss her, but he holds her hand and says, 'Young lady, wake up.' And she does, to the astonishment of everybody, and the great joy of her parents.

Villains in the family

It is not always a giant or demon who is the chief villain in pantomime. Think of *Cinderella*. It is Cinderella's stepmother and stepsisters, members of her own family, who are the cruel villains. They certainly don't understand that love is the secret of happy family life. They think they can be happy by bullying and being cruel to their gentle stepsister and making her life a misery. But Jesus Christ sat on a mountainside and said, 'Blessed are the meek, for they shall inherit the earth.' And at the end it is meek Cinders who marries Prince Charming and lives happily ever after.

The hero or the heroine of every pantomime has to learn from their experiences. Often when the story begins they are far from heroic, and sometimes rather stupid. But they learn from their mistakes, and then they live happily ever after. Even sweet innocent Cinderella was weeping helplessly while the Ugly Sisters went to the Royal Ball, and she had to learn from her Fairy Godmother not to be a helpless victim, to use her imagination, to be brave and go to the ball on her own.

Aladdin and his Wonderful Lamp, one of the stories from *The Arabian Nights*, is another story where the villain is a member of the family – wicked Uncle Abanazer. Aladdin is a daydreamer, the son of a poor, overworked mother who runs a Chinese laundry. He is of little help to poor old Widow Twanky (or Nora Twanky as she is known when I play her!). Aladdin has fallen in love and wants to marry the beautiful Princess Lotus Flower, but of course he is far too poor to ever hope to meet her. Wicked Uncle Abanazer is an unscrupulous magician. He tricks Aladdin into going into a cave to find treasure, but when he's got the gold, he leaves Aladdin locked in the cave to die.

Aladdin finds a tatty old lamp in the cave, and when he rubs it, a genie of the lamp appears and grants him three wishes. It's a resurrection story. In a hopeless, dark situation, left to die, Aladdin is saved when he rubs the lamp, which is similar to praying. The Genie of the lamp is the Holy Spirit who comes to us when we pray. Aladdin learns from the Genie not to put all his trust in idle dreams of treasure, but to become good and courageous and generous. So Aladdin is able to escape from the cave, he meets the beautiful princess who falls in love with him, and they all live happily ever after.

Beauty is only skin deep

In some way every pantomime principal has to learn something about themselves, and change, before they can outwit their own particular giant or demon. In nearly every case it is the Principal Boy or Principal Girl, but in the story of *Mother Goose*, it is the Dame who has the important lesson to learn.

Mother Goose, through vanity, makes a pact with the Wicked Demon to part with her goose that lays the golden eggs in exchange for becoming beautiful. She gives him her goose and goes to bathe in a magic fountain. It's a bit like a weird sort of baptism. She emerges looking beautiful but finds that now she is changed, nobody loves her, even her own son, Silly Billy, because she is no longer his kind, ugly Mother Goose. She has to learn that appearances aren't everything, that beauty is only skin deep, and that it can't make you happy. A good fairy makes her ugly again, but lovely inside, so she and Silly Billy are a happy family again. This is fundamental Christian teaching – that what is in your heart is more important than how you appear on the outside.

Don't you think that is a good moral story for so many young girls today who will do anything to be thin and beautiful? They refuse to eat normally, they take drugs, and they will do almost anything – which is the same thing as

Mother Goose making a pact with a demon – in exchange for what they think is a beautiful body. What you must look after is the only really beautiful part of yourself, the 'inner you' that can give and receive love.

Dame Nora

Nora Batty has ensured that I get more offers than I can accept to play Dame Nora in pantomime every Christmas. Sometimes I might be a Flying Fairy Godmother or the Queen, or Mother Goose, but very often I am simply Dame Nora.

Working on *Last of the Summer Wine* for the past twenty-five years has meant that I have only been able to accept a limited amount of theatre work, which has sometimes been a big disappointment. However, I nearly always manage to do a pantomime for a few weeks in December and January, which means I haven't completely lost the pleasure of working in front of a live audience, which all actors love. Pantomime audiences are especially lovely. They haven't come to be critics, they've come to enjoy themselves, and join in, and although it is hard work I always thoroughly enjoy myself too.

When I first started in pantomime, which isn't so many years ago, the pantomime would always begin with all the dancers dancing on the village green or round a maypole, or something cheerful and bright like that. It gave the small children in the audience a chance to get used to looking at the big stage with all the movement, and listening to the music which is louder than on TV at home.

40

It's different these days, and I think it's a pity. They always seem to begin in the dark, and then there's a huge bang and a flash and the Wicked Demon appears making scary threats. Small children who have never been to the theatre before are terrified. They are used to watching a little box in the corner of the living room. They come to the theatre, and the size of the stage and the sound of the orchestra are overwhelming enough. But when it's all dark – and most little children are afraid in the dark – and then there's a terrific flash and this villain appears, they are absolutely terrified. I've seen so many families distraught, because one little girl has had to come out because she's so frightened, and one little boy is left in, and the poor mother hasn't known what to do!

The boy who never grew up

Peter Pan is about a boy who refuses to grow up. In order never to grow up, he has to avoid normal family life and live in Never-Never Land. This is true of so many people who choose not to marry and settle down – particularly men – bachelors who remain little boys, even when they are old, fat and bald! We all know Peter Pans in real life. Wendy comes to understand that although life in Never-Never Land is exciting, it isn't until you accept your role in real family life, and allow yourself to grow up, that you find happiness.

In *Peter Pan*, even though Captain Hook is punished by being eaten by the crocodile, he is swallowed alive by the crocodile. He's all in one piece – a bit like Jonah and the Whale. And that's in Never-Never Land. When the children fly home to London, Captain Hook is Mr Darling, their father, and he is so sorry for what he has done that he has moved into the dog's kennel.

Love is stronger than death

One of the traditional parts of a pantomime is when the comic lead, or sometimes it is the Principal Boy, asks the children to tell him when the villain is about. While they are talking, the giant or demon is creeping up behind them, and the children all begin to shout out: 'He's behind you!'

The actor pretends not to hear them, and they shout and scream louder and louder, and then, of course, when the actor does turn round, there's nobody there. So he tells the audience off for making it up. It's great fun, because everyone joins in, mums and dads included, and the whole family is participating in trying to save the stupid person on the stage.

In a pantomime, good always triumphs over evil in the end. Always. Likewise, Jesus taught that love is a light that will shine on in the darkness and triumph over darkness and evil.

The actors on the stage can see the children, and you can tell they really hate the villain. We say, 'What shall we do to him?' They all scream, 'Kill him! Kill him!' I usually say, 'Now I know what we'll do that's better than that. We'll make him good!' You never kill him, because good cannot kill evil; you've got to transform it, make the villain into a good person. And this is the story of all pantomimes.

STRATEGIES FOR CHARACTER BUILDING

* Read the Bible – start with the two books
  of Samuel and the two books of Kings.

* Discover your own inner strength for
  fighting giants.

* Pride and selfishness will never win you the
  heart of Prince or Princess Charming.

* Beauty is only skin deep.

* Sometimes it is in your darkest hour that
  you will find your heart's desire.

* There is hope and forgiveness for everyone.

'Many waters cannot quench love; rivers cannot wash it away' (*Song of Songs 8:7, NIV*).

4
THE DEALER

The rules of the game have been perused, the counters have been placed in the Counters Pool and the cards have been got out of their box. But who is to be the Dealer?

It is the faith and experience of my family that the Dealer has always been, is, and always will be, God. Nothing has ever happened in my life, happy or sad, that has ever led me to doubt this.

Letting go and letting God

These days I am quite often asked to speak or to be interviewed about the Christian faith, but I always feel I'm not trained or qualified to speak about it. I haven't studied Christianity as a subject. I only know what I have personally experienced, and how I feel. In acting terms you could say that I'm an enthusiastic amateur.

So I always ask for God's assistance to say the right

things. I would hate to upset people by saying the wrong things. I ask him if he would just put it into my mind what I should say, and he seems to. Suddenly I find ideas and thoughts coming into my mind, and I think, 'Yes, that's it.' I find I can talk about things in the Bible, and explain them in my own way, and it seems to come out all right. But it's God's doing, not mine, I'm quite sure of that.

If someone who doesn't believe tells me about something that is troubling them, I know that it's no good preaching to them. You just have to listen. Give them the love and comfort that God would give them, even if it has to be without them knowing that the love comes from God.

Money can't buy you love

God is the Dealer, but sometimes he deals you cards that you don't want. As Christians we pray, 'Thy will not mine be done'. But it isn't always easy. Although life is full of many blessings, there can also be disappointments and pain to bear.

Katherine, our oldest daughter, found that she couldn't have children a few years after she married. It was a great sadness for us all, and especially for her. She tried IVF treatment, but when that didn't work after three attempts on the NHS, she felt that it was God's will that she shouldn't have children and has accepted it. Our youngest daughter, Susan, is forty and unmarried. She may well marry one day, but it is unlikely now that she will have any children when she does.

Which also means that John and I won't have any

grandchildren. When I see Con helping with her two grandchildren, and my cousin Fran, with her four, and our best friends, Jim and Sheila, who have six grandchildren, I know they've got a kind of happiness that no amount of money and success can buy. They are truly blessed with their grandchildren.

I have to admit that sometimes I feel sad that John and I won't be grandparents, but when I have had so many other blessings in my life, I hope I am not so churlish as to complain. You are not protected from troubles as a Christian, but you do get great comfort from saying prayers and speaking to God about your sadness.

Standing at the foot of the cross.

Families, close families, can be a cause of sadness as well as joy. We've already seen how a 'black sheep' can cause a lot of trouble in the pantomime stories, and they exist in real life too. It is especially sad when members of the same family won't speak to one another, especially when it is because of something that happened so long ago that nobody can remember exactly what it was.

Even when there are no 'villains' in the family, there is the great sadness you feel when something happens to hurt one of your own chicks. When you love someone, you suffer almost as much as they do when things go wrong. It can be worse watching someone else suffer than suffering yourself, and when it's your child, you wish you could take the trouble from them and bear it yourself.

As your children grow into young men and women, you sometimes have to watch them having their hearts broken by a failed romance, or a broken marriage, and that nearly breaks your heart too.

The worst time for us came in 1991, when our daughter Katherine found she had a lump on her breast. At first she thought it was still the hormone treatment that was taking time to settle down after the IVF, so it was a week or two before she went to see her doctor. He sent her to a specialist, who told her that 90 per cent of the time these little lumps turn out to be nothing serious. But to be on the safe side he would remove the lump, and he'd let her know as soon as the results came back from the laboratory.

I was about to go away on tour, taking over from Peggy Mount the part of Madam Arcati in *Blithe Spirit*, which meant travelling up to Inverness for a week. When we arrived in Inverness on Tuesday, the landlady at our Bed and Breakfast said, 'You've got a letter.' It was from Katherine, and in it she said, 'While you're up there, you have to see the following things … ' She knew the area well, and she had listed where we had to go every day, and all the things she wanted us to see. She had suggested something different for each day of the week we would be there.

We opened on Tuesday night. When John came to collect me after the performance he said, 'Susan's been on the phone. They're rushing Katherine into hospital in the morning to operate again. It's cancer.'

That has been the worst moment of my life. Our first impulse was to get on a plane the next morning and rush straight home. After great deliberations all night – neither of us slept – we decided to telephone Katherine first thing in the morning to see what she wanted us to do.

I telephoned her early the next day, and there was no reply. I knew Susan had gone straight over to be with her, so I couldn't understand why nobody answered. We kept on ringing the number all morning. I was beside myself. I said to John, 'I don't know where she is. Where can she have gone? She should be there, getting ready.'

Finally, at nearly midday, we got through and as soon as I heard her voice I found myself crying, 'Oh Katherine! Where have you been?'

She sounded completely calm. She said, 'It's Wednesday morning. Susan and I have been to St Mark's, to the midweek communion service.'

I told her I wanted to drop everything and come home to be with her. She said, 'Certainly not. I shall be in good hands. I have a specialist here who I have every faith in. Susan is with me. You must stay there. You must do just exactly what I've told you to do in my letter, and go to all those places on my list.'

So that's what we did. We kept to her list and did all the things she'd told us to do. I don't know how, and I can't remember anything much about any of them, but we did them. I didn't dare tell anybody in the company, because if somebody had started being sympathetic I don't think I could have carried on. It was without doubt the hardest week I have ever lived through.

Katherine was coming home on the Sunday, so we drove straight down from Inverness early that morning and arrived at the hospital at exactly three o'clock, visiting time. We rushed in wanting to scoop her up and take her home, but she said, 'Oh well, I think I'll have my tea here before coming out.'

The specialist told us, 'She's the sort of patient we love. You just feed her, and she gets better.'

She had to go back for courses of radiation and

chemotherapy, but we seemed to have turned the corner. It's over eight years ago now, and she is keeping very well. She only has to go back once a year for a check-up. I thank the Lord for helping us through it all.

In the end, the good that comes from belonging to a family, the happiness and the love, far outweigh any sadness. And even the sadness itself, when you've been through difficult times together and helped one another come through, becomes part of a very deep bond that can never be broken.

Good Friday

Jesus' family, his mother and many of his closest friends on earth, had to stand by and watch him dying, nailed to the cross. It is hard to imagine anything more terrible. I don't really understand why it is called Good Friday. It was Tragic Friday.

Each year, I pray that it will go dark on Good Friday. Then perhaps people might realise what a sad day it is, instead of spending the day at garden centres and funfairs. Everything is open on Good Friday in Ashton. It's just like any Bank Holiday. They have a big fair.

Some of Ashton's Christians hold a parade to Daisy Nook, just outside the town, carrying a huge cross, to try to bring home to people what Good Friday is all about. And I always think at around three o'clock, when we are coming to the end of the three-hour service, 'Oh, I hope it goes dark.' Then people would say, 'What's happened?'

As Susan says, it was no use her praying, as she did when she was little girl, 'Oh! Please don't let him die!' He had to die in order to show us not to fear death, and he rose again so we would understand that dying is only a part of living, a step on our journey. I still do wonder, 'Why did he have to suffer so much?' But then again, I know of many people, when they have been in great physical pain, who have been grateful to know that God understands well what bodily pain is like.

Life after death

The surest thing in life is death. Some people believe that when you die, that's it, you've gone. It's over. But I firmly believe that Jesus Christ has promised us that if we have faith, if we believe, then there is life after death. After the crucifixion, the cruellest death anyone could suffer, Jesus rose from the dead and people saw him. He said to them, 'Fear not. Only believe.' So I do. I firmly believe in life after death. I don't know what form it will take, but I believe that it will happen.

I believe that it will be really wonderful. So many people look so peaceful as they pass away, almost smiling. I think they must see something. John's mother seemed to be seeing and communicating with members of her family during her last few days, as though they had been sent to lead her. She looked absolutely transformed and lovely when she died. I don't know that I believe in hell or people burning in fires. I can't really believe in that. I think some people make their own hell on earth. Nobody knows. But if you have faith, Jesus has promised us eternal life. We don't know how it will be, but if we have faith, then there is nothing to fear.

Keeping Sunday special

I'm a great believer that Sundays should be kept as a special family day. I think families need a day that they can spend together, all at home at the same time. If all the shops are open, that not only means that people will spend their time shopping instead of being at home, it also means there are people working in the shops. So they can't be with their families, either. I know the supermarkets say, 'We don't force anyone to work on Sunday.' But I think a lot of people feel forced to work, because they are afraid that if they don't agree, they could be sacked. There's so much pressure. I don't agree with it at all.

There are so many things open now on Sundays: leisure centres with their swimming pools and slimming classes, martial arts lessons and sports stadiums – all open on Sundays. They even hold major football matches. Did you hear about the vicar in Birmingham with a church next to the Stadium, who decided to ring the church bells – Bong! Bong! Bong! – all the way through the big match whenever there was a Sunday morning kick-off? It was one way to remind people what they were missing!

I am convinced that Sunday should be a family day, whether they go to church or not, when everyone is at home on the same day. So often these days Mother is working on one shift, say from eight until two, and Father's on another shift. The children are at school all day from Monday to Friday. So many children come home from school and their parents aren't home and you've only the weekend when you can all be together. There's no hope for family life when people are working all hours, and such pressures don't make for any kind of happy family life.

Unfortunately, even for me, I often have to do

performances on a Sunday when I'm working in pantomime. I used to refuse to work on a Sunday, but I don't now. I've given in to the majority. But last Christmas, doing *Aladdin* in Hull, we only had to work one Sunday in the whole run. I told the theatre manager how delighted I was and he said that it really wasn't for any religious reason, but he found out it cost him so much – the whole of the staff had to be paid double – that it just wasn't worth it.

I thought, Hurrah! Perhaps more people will come round to realising this, and we can go back to Sunday being a special day. It's a bit like the abolition of the slave trade – people protested about the cruelty of it for years, but it was only when it stopped being economical that it was finally abolished.

What my sister Connie wrote in my autograph book

> When the elevator to success has stopped
> Don't sit down
> Try the stairs.
> C. Higginbottom 15.7.42

The escalator

I have been given a life that I could never have envisaged at all. God lifted me out of the typing pool, and put me in the right place at the right time. I've never fought for work.It's all just snowballed, from walk-ons, to little bit parts, to bigger parts, to leading lady. I've never been ambitious or gone out of my way to get on. I know that I have been extremely fortunate and blessed.

Even Nora Batty was like a present from God. We had just come back from a holiday in Spain, arriving home in the early hours, and the family had all gone straight up to bed. I got up at about noon to put the washing-machine on, and the telephone rang. It was my agent saying that the BBC would like to see me that very day. I said, 'I've just come back from holiday. I can't go all the way back down to London today.' She said, 'No, they are holding the interviews in Manchester.'

I went along quite reluctantly for the last appointment of the day with the great comedy director, Jimmy Gilbert. He was casting a new series to be called Last of the Summer Wine. He was only in Manchester for that one day. If he had been there the day before, I wouldn't have been seen. Someone else would have played Nora. It's been like that all along.

The only disadvantage of being in a long-running series like Summer Wine has been that I have not been able to do as much theatre work as I would have liked. As I've said, I always enjoy the pantomime season at Christmas, but for the rest of the year I've not been able to be in any play that is planning a long run.

Trying the stairs

Some years after Summer Wine began, I was offered a twelve-month contract in the West End of London. I knew there was no way I could do it, because of the number of weeks we spend filming Summer Wine – which has been the case for the past twenty-odd years for me.

However, on this occasion, we were all sitting on the location bus in Yorkshire eating sandwiches, and Alan

Bell, who directs *Summer Wine* came and sat next to me. That doesn't often happen. I said to him, quite casually, and really just to make conversation, 'I've just had to refuse a job in the West End.'

He said, 'What in?'

I said, 'They offered me the part of the daily lady, Mrs Northrop, in *When We are Married* at the Whitehall. Of course I've said I can't do it, because of the filming here.'

'Oh!' Alan said, 'You mustn't do that. Get back on to them right away and say you *can* do it.'

'What do you mean? How can I?'

He said, 'We'll work round you. You drive back up here every Saturday night, and we'll film all your scenes on Sunday and Monday up to lunchtime. Then you can drive back to London and do the play for the rest of the week.'

And this is what I did. Now, I'd not tried to make it possible. I thought it *wasn't* possible. It was sheer chance that I had been sitting next to Alan Bell and mentioned it at all. But it worked out. No actress likes to pass up the chance of working in the West End of London.

It was hard work, though. It was very tiring for John too, because he was doing all the driving. After a Saturday night performance we would sometimes arrive home from London in the early hours of the morning. On one occasion we were stopped by a policeman at 2 a.m. and he asked us where we were going.

Without any hesitation, John replied, 'I'm driving my wife home from work!'

STRATEGIES FOR THE DEALER

* Say your prayers – let God help you with your life.

* Count your blessings (again!).

* 'Standing by' sometimes means standing by a cross.

* Keep Sunday a special family day.

* Accept life as it comes.

* When opportunities come your way – seize them.

'... Lo, I am with you alway, even unto the end of the world' (*Matthew 28:20, AV*).

5
THE PLAYERS
(ANY NUMBER OVER TWO)

Happy Families is a game for three or more players. In other words, for it to be a 'Happy Family' it is not enough for there just to be two people who are in love. There have to be others.

I don't mean you've got to have children before you count as a family. But somehow there has to be at least three of you. I know it's unusual nowadays for grandparents, parents, in-laws, brothers and sisters, uncles, aunts, nephews and nieces all to live near one another in the same neighbourhood in the way we did when I was young. But today it is much easier to keep in touch. Hardly anybody had a telephone, for instance, when I was a child.

Knocking on the wall

You used to knock on the wall. Expectant mothers, when their time had come, would knock on the wall, and their neighbour, who would have been waiting for the signal, would dash round to the midwife's house. There was far less feeling of isolation and loneliness in those days. There was always somebody around. You got to know people so much better because you all popped in and out of each other's homes – not just having the occasional word over the garden wall.

The London Cockneys used to do this, in their little old houses, before they were moved out to Dagenham or up into high-rise blocks. People now are much richer, and they've become more private, somehow. They don't trust one another like they used to. They've stopped feeling part of a community of people, like a neighbourhood family. I always think it's very strange when people telephone their next-door neighbour about something. I always think – well, why don't they call round? And have contact? Why don't they just go out of their front door and say hello?

I remember (well, no, I don't remember, because although I was there, I was a tiny baby, but I have been told this tale many times) the occasion that my mother got double pneumonia, which means it was in both lungs. She became so ill that she passed out. Connie was there, but she was not quite three, because it was shortly after I was born. Poor little Connie was alone in the house with a baby sister and her mother in a dead faint. She tried to knock on the wall for the lady next door, with her little soft, baby fingers. Because that was what you did. Even at two, Connie knew that if she kept on knocking, someone would come. She would have seen my mother do it. It was what everybody did. That was how your neighbours were. If you needed anything, if it was serious, you would knock on the wall.

Eventually the neighbours heard this soft little tapping sound. It must have sounded like a mouse. They came round to see what was wrong, and saw my mother on the floor and got the doctor.

A similar thing happened to Auntie Nellie, who was once engaged to Uncle Leonard. We always thought of her as 'Auntie' Nellie even though she never really was an aunt because Uncle Leonard was killed in the First World War, so they never married. Auntie Nellie eventually married someone else and during the Second World War they moved to York. She was on her own when she was suddenly taken very ill. She was sitting on a chair near to a built-in wall cupboard. She was just conscious enough to keep knocking the cupboard door, banging it open and shut, until a neighbour heard it and came running round. So the doctor was fetched for her. Hardly anyone had, or needed, a telephone in those days.

I think it still happens in little pockets, but it's the exception rather than the rule. In the village of Padfield, not far from us, there are some rows of little old houses. If there are any elderly people still living in them from years ago, I'm sure they still knock on the wall to one another.

Mrs Kirk

There are people who become such a part of the household that they become additional members of your family. Like our Mrs Kirk.

I first knew Mrs Kirk when I was a child, because she used to work at the vicarage for Mr Edward Porter Tyson, and always attended church. Years later, one of her sons became Mayor of Dukinfield, and he still attends St Mark's. A few years after we were married, John and I moved back into Dukinfield in order to be near my mother so I could help her with my father when he had his attacks. We had bought quite a big four-bedroom house and the children were both small, so I asked Mrs Kirk if she would come and help us.

She lived in a cottage nearby and readily agreed. Nobody could clean a house like Mrs Kirk. She was absolutely amazing. She moved the wardrobes and all the sofas and chairs into the middle of the room to 'do behind'. If ever we wanted to go out in the evening, and my mother was accompanying us, Mrs Kirk would come and sit with the children. The girls loved her.

We all loved Mrs Kirk. She was part of the family. But she was getting on in years even then, and she has passed away now, God rest her.

The Christian family ...

And then you have the great Christian family. If you can find a church to belong to, even if you don't have a family of your own, you will soon understand what family life is like. You will become part of an instant extended family, a family that anyone can belong to. If you find the right church for you, it is like being a member of a huge and happy, hard-working family, working for the neighbourhood.

Mothering Sunday is the day we give thanks for our Mother Church, not just our own mothers. That's what it is, our Mother Church. Traditionally, anyone who had moved away from their homes, for whatever reason, would return to their birthplace on Mothering Sunday, and go to the church they were baptised in.

I like the way baptisms are usually done these days, when they take place as part of the regular Sunday service, in front of the whole congregation, not just as small private gatherings on a Sunday afternoon. In baptism we all want to welcome the new little Christian into our church family.

If you are churchgoers, finding a church gets you started when you move to another town. It's the first step to becoming part of your new community. Wherever you go, there are Christians there. It's not the same as your original family or church, but it can become so if you give it time. At least you are in there. It's then up to you to go and give as much to the church as you will get out of it.

Not *all* churches have got their act together to make a newcomer feel welcome, but many have. Don't be put off. Sometimes it's not because they aren't glad to see you, but because they are themselves shy or not sure if you want to be approached. So you have to work at it, like everything else.

Working at it

It was the Christian Church that originally started so many things that we take for granted now, like hospitals and schools. Today most churches are still right at the centre of community life. Belonging to the church family gives you a focus, helps you decide what to do with your life, and it can give you a role in the community, bring you into contact with other people in your village or town.

It depends what your talents are. You might be asked to help with 'meals on wheels' or delivering parish magazines if you have a car. Or you might be asked if you would like to join the choir if you can read music. Or to organise a coffee morning in your home to raise funds. Contribute to an annual flower festival. Distribute offerings after the Harvest Festival. Cook for the parish Harvest Supper. Welcome visitors to the church. Visit local people who are unwell and read to them or help them with their shopping.

Whatever your talents are, you can be sure they will be used. And even if you are old and battered and think you don't have any talents, you can still pray for the work of the church. This is the main thing – you are part of a community of prayer who love and support each other.

I've heard people say, 'I read my Bible at home and sing along with the hymns on *Songs of Praise* on Sunday night.' Or, 'I can worship God when I go out in the garden.' But I think they should remember these words of Jesus, 'When two or three are gathered together in my name, I will grant their request.' That means to me that we are asked to come together to pray. That's what the Church is for.

Finding the right church

A lady wrote to me, after reading my autobiography, telling me how alone in the world she was; she had nobody, and she was so lonely. She had tried going to a church, but when she was there nobody spoke to her and she felt even worse. Could I help her in any way?

My advice was that she should try to find a church where they encourage Bible study or prayer groups, held in different people's homes. Everyone is welcome. It's easier to get to know people you meet in a small group sitting in a normal home, rather than in a pew in a big church and just seeing the backs of people's heads. Or milling about in a big crowd at the end of the service, where if you are shy it is difficult to know what to say.

In these groups they usually read the Bible and discuss what they've read, and then they pray together. I suppose in a way we're getting back to the first Christians. Jesus used to go to different houses and sit and talk to the family and guests who were there. So in a way I feel these small house groups are getting back to our roots.

The lady hasn't written back saying it didn't work, so I am hoping she has found what she needs.

Some churches, as I've said, are not very good at welcoming new people. But if you find the kind of church that our daughter Susan works in, an ecumenical group, where Anglicans, Methodists, Baptists and Catholics all work together, then I'm sure that most people would find it very welcoming.

I once said to Susan, when she first started out as a curate at an ecumenical centre in Kent, 'And how do you know which are the Anglicans and which are the Methodists?' And she said, 'I don't know and I don't ask. They are all my parishioners, and it doesn't matter what they are.'

It's similar at Milton Keynes, where she is now a vicar, but her church is a fourteenth-century building, which doesn't lend itself so easily to the ecumenical approach. Yet there are four of them working together in the ecumenical team, in three churches. The Team Rector has another old fourteenth-century church, and there's a brand-new church, Christ the King, which the Roman Catholics and Baptists share. The Team Rector, Susan, the Baptist minister and the Roman Catholic priest all work together, moving round and taking services in one another's churches. It's a team ministry. Obviously Susan can't lead Mass in the Roman Catholic church, so instead she administers a blessing to the congregation. Yet her team do try to have as many ecumenical services as possible which are non-Eucharist and therefore in which they can all participate. This is especially important on Good Friday, when they have joint ecumenical services in each of the churches.

Palaver and top show

I was brought up in the Church of England, and we are used to wearing robes. Even at St Mark's – which I would describe as 'low' rather than 'high' church, so we don't go in for 'smells and bells' – the choir is robed, and the vicar has an altar server, who is my cousin Fran's grandson, Richard. (In a recent official photograph to mark the church's 150th anniversary, you could see Richard's trainers under his robes!) But sometimes I feel that we are going in for rather a lot of palaver and top show.

I sometimes wonder if we're making the same mistake as they did in the days of Christ, when he turned over the tables of the money changers and said, 'This is a house of prayer. And you've turned it into a den of thieves.'

There's quite a lot of commercial activity allowed in churches these days, coffee shops and books stalls and art exhibitions (particularly in cathedrals), although I do realise that money is needed to keep them open. Those ancient buildings cost a fortune to heat and light, let alone the repairs. Which brings me to another thing I feel should be changed ...

Paying for the upkeep of churches and cathedrals

I don't agree with churches charging anybody to go in. Some churches and cathedrals won't allow you in until you've paid an entrance fee. I just can't accept that; to me the house of God is a place of prayer and must be open to everybody. If you are asked for a donation and you can afford it, then you can pay.

Nevertheless, these ancient stone buildings cost unbelievable amounts of money to maintain. Some of the ways they've thought of to raise donations have been ingenious. York Minster used to ask for voluntary donations to pay for a minute of the cathedral's life. At some other places, like the Boston Stump, if you make a donation you can have the church floodlit for a night, to celebrate a family anniversary or some other occasion.

A lot of pressure would be taken off cathedrals if city councils would take on part of the responsibility for keeping them maintained and open. If a town or city has a cathedral or a beautiful ancient church, visitors will come from all over the world to see it. Over the centuries they have been places of pilgrimage, and who can say how many prayers have been answered? York receives thousands of visitors every year because York Minster is such an attraction. And then there's Chester Cathedral ... And Lichfield. They are great repositories, too, of marvellous works of art. They all draw people into the city, and yet the city council doesn't pay anything towards the upkeep. I think this is wrong ...

But I'm getting rather away from Happy Families, aren't I? Perhaps I should have a word with Mr Chip the Carpenter. I'm sure he'll have friends with influence on the town council!

Workmates

If you work in one place or one profession for many years, your workmates can become 'one of the family'. By 'family', I mean anyone whose life becomes entangled with yours.

In acting, this happens in some jobs, and not in others. In *Crossroads*, everyone came to feel like family. I have many friends for life from working in *Crossroads*. It's not been quite the same with *Last of the Summer Wine*, even though I've worked in this series for a lot longer. Apart from Jane, and Thora, who I've admired all my life and feel very privileged to be working with now, I wouldn't say I was really close to anyone. I wouldn't even say Bill Owen and I were ever very close, but we did try to stick up for each other when they ask too much of us.

Bill's part was very active – when you think that he was eighty-five. He really had to come up those steps to my door. Very often, when we started he'd say, 'Now look – this has got to be a take. I can't keep going up and down those steps.' But he often had to.

In one of the most recent series, Compo wants Nora to sew a button on his shirt cuff, so I make him push his hand through the letterbox rather than have him in the house. But it was so difficult, to get his arm through. He had to kneel for ages on the stone step – and it's not as though he were a young man. It would have been difficult for anybody.

Also in the most recent series, a man decides to form 'Robin Hood and his Merry Men', and when Compo finds out that there could be food attached to it, he decides to become a Merry Man. At the end of it he gets fastened up in a tree, and he's hanging upside down, and I'm standing looking up at him, and he says, 'Ee, Cleggy? Now I know which knee Nora's scar is on.'

When I first read the script I could hardly believe it. I thought, 'Well, I don't know how we're going to do this.' For the long shot, when he shoots up the tree, of course they had his 'stand-in'. But then they said to us, 'Now it's you and Bill.'

I said to Bill in the car, 'You're not going to really do this, are you?'

He said, 'But what can I do?'

I said, 'Bill. You really will have to tell them. You are eighty-five and you cannot hang upside down from the branch of a tree.'

He said, 'Well, I said to Alan "It's going to be very difficult …"'

I said, 'Ring Roy Clarke and tell him. Say, "Look, Roy, I know these ideas are very funny, but I just can't do them."'

I mean, I'm nowhere near eighty-five, but I couldn't hang upside down in a tree.

But Bill did it! We did two or three takes of him seeing my knee while he was hanging upside down from the tree. You can't help feeling affection for someone as daft as that. Bill was eighty-five and in the middle of filming the next series when he died, and I know that that was exactly how he would have wanted it to be.

Lives become enmeshed, and it can sometimes be painful, but in the end it is all about love, and that's really all that this book is about.

Love is a fire that kindling its first embers in the narrow nook of a private bosom, caught from a wandering spark out of another private heart, glows and enlarges until it warms and beams upon multitudes of men and women, upon the universal heart of all, and so lights up the whole world and nature with generous flames.

Ralph Emerson

STRATEGIES FOR THE PLAYERS

* Remember that 'family' means anyone whose life is tangled up with yours.

* Invite neighbours into your home – don't just wave at them occasionally.

* Keep in touch with family and friends by letter and telephone.

* Become part of the church family.

* Give of your time and talents, and share in the joy of 'belonging' in your own home community.

* Extend your 'family' through friendship, through neighbours, through people at work.

'A friend loves at all times, and a brother is born for adversity' (*Proverbs 17:17, NIV*).

6
PLAYING THE GAME

Everyone has assembled, the tokens are in the Counters Pool, and the Dealer has given each Player his hand of cards, so now it is time for the game of Happy Families to begin. The purpose of the game is to collect as many complete Happy Families as you can – or in my game, as many completely Happy Families as you can!

Playing the game in life is how to help members of your own family thrive and help each other through all the good times, the bad times, the happy times, the sad times, the irritating times. I was dealt the hand of a large extended family, and part of that deal is that you have to learn about sharing from a very early age.

The Best Christmas Present in the World (Ever)

I am often asked if I would donate something from my own childhood to auction for charity – like an old teddy bear or a doll. The sad truth is, I haven't got a single one left. It's not that I didn't have some wonderful toys. We didn't have a lot of money, but my parents were both very good at making things, and one year, when I was about eight or nine, I had the best Christmas present any little girl could ever wish for. It was a little draper's shop. My father made it with real wood, not just hardboard or anything that wouldn't last. It was beautiful, solid wood, painted green. The doorknob was a bead. The sign on the front said, 'M. Higginbottom, Draper'.

You could always tell we were a family, because my mother would buy a length of material and make herself a dress, and then make one each for Connie and me out of the same material, so the three of us often wore identical dresses. Even when we walked along the prom at Blackpool, far from home, anyone could tell that we were The Family, out together. For my shop, my mother had made several sweet little dresses, and she had put tiny rolls of material on matchsticks, so they looked absolutely authentic.

It wasn't just that the shop itself was beautiful, it was all the trouble and care – all the love that lay behind the making of it and the giving of it, and I thought it was the best little shop in the world.

But then the war came.

It wasn't only clothes we had to hand down to our many young cousins during the war, it was our toys as well. That was hard. I had a very special doll. She had a lovely bisque face. Off she went, in her pram, to one of the Bainbridge cousins, never to be seen again.

Even if you were 'a cut above', like our cousins the Gregsons, you still couldn't find presents for your children at Christmas during the war years, for love nor money. Auntie Alice Gregson's daughter, Anne, when she was about nine or ten, wanted a 'shop'. My mum and dad said, 'Oh well, we've got a shop. You can have our Minnie's old shop. You can replenish the things.'

So Anne got my shop. I think they turned it into a confectioner's shop for her. I know I was fourteen by then, and probably wasn't playing with it much, but I was very sad to see it go. And even now, when I think about it, I still wish I could have kept it. It would have been a family heirloom. I don't know what happened to it eventually. Perhaps I should put an advert in the paper for it: has anybody seen this shop?

So when I think back to my childhood, I've only my memories. No worn-out old bear with a button eye, no doll, no 'M. Higginbottom, Draper' shop. But in some ways, perhaps that's how it should be. I probably remember such possessions more fondly, and better, than I ever would if I'd kept them and they'd mouldered away in the back of a toy cupboard. Instead, they were loved and played with by generations of children. And because I had the pain of parting with them, they stay very vividly in my memory.

Children who have too much

Buying children's clothes is so expensive. Surely a tiny little shoe shouldn't cost as much as a shoe to fit me? But it does. If ever our two girls complained when they were young about not having things other children had, or Susan grumbled about having to wear Katherine's hand-me-downs, I would say, 'We are four people living on one person's wage. As my mother always used to say: "You must cut your coat according to your cloth."'

There is far too much instant gratification these days and not enough working up to things gradually. Television is a lot to blame for this; they put so much temptation in front of your eyes. Summer is barely over and immediately they are pushing things at you to buy for Christmas. So many wonderful things are advertised on television and the children think they must have them. And so many of these things are dreadfully expensive. They aren't advertising a little drum and two sticks – it's the full electronic keyboard!

I think many children today have far too much too early on in life, and by the time they are sixteen or seventeen they are looking for something different, some new excitement, and that is when they often turn to drugs – because they have already been given *everything*. Often in pantomime, when the comedian does the song sheet with the audience, all the little children – four-, five- and six-year olds – come up on stage and he says to all of them, 'What did Father Christmas bring you this year?'

I hear so many of them whisper back, 'A computer'! What is there left in life to strive for if they've already got a computer at that age? There's nowhere else for them to go. Parents spend far too much money on their children. They say, 'Oh well, they've got to have it. All the other children at school have one.' That's a load of rubbish! They *don't* all have one. We are spoiling our children, giving them far too many things. So when they get to sixteen, what else is there? They've tried smoking, alcohol, probably sex. So many of them turn to drugs, and sometimes it kills them. How many times have you read in the papers about a teenager being killed after taking their first Ecstasy tablet? Why don't they see the danger?

How can we get back to family life? How can we set a better example and show how a good family life can make all the difference? I get so worried when I read the news. What was it last week? Nurses saying that children of eleven should be given the 'morning after' pill. Children of *eleven*! Without their parents' knowledge! This is all wrong. Parents should be responsible for their children, but this sort of thing is taking the responsibility away from them.

On being a mother

Parenthood is the one job none of us are trained for. That and being an MP. The two most important jobs in the country – bringing up children, and helping to run the country – and you don't have to have any training at all. Any old MP, who is voted in because he or she has got a nice face, can suddenly find himself or herself made Chancellor of the Exchequer, making decisions about everybody's money.

Being a mother is something most of us have no training for either, and it is just as important. When I was in hospital having my two babies – they kept me in for ten days each time because both my daughters were breach babies with extended legs, so it was difficult – I saw lots of other girls also becoming mothers for the first time. Some girls took to it like a duck to water, as I did, but others really were stressed out. They were in tears over this, and in tears over that, and they were so tense that their milk couldn't flow, and their baby would cry and that made things even worse. They were in a state of shock and it took them quite a few days before they were able to relax and enjoy their babies. Most of them got there in the end, but having your baby is only the beginning of all the things you've got to learn about being a parent.

Learning from older family members

I think I learned how to be a mother from having a wonderful mother myself. You can learn all sorts of things from other members of your family. You can watch the older generations, your grandparents, your parents, and also your brothers and sisters, and see how they cope with different situations you may not have met yet. Then you've got a model to base yourself on – or to throw out if you think they made too many mistakes! It is how you learn and grow.

It can sometimes be painful – having to stand by and watch someone you love suffering, or a beloved parent or grandparent facing old age and death – but this too is part of good family life. Just by being there you are actually helping them, and making them feel loved and supported. And if you have seen other members of your family going through sad or painful experiences, it seems to make it easier when your own time comes.

Spending time together

It was a very happy time, both when we were children, and when our children were young, but it is so hard to describe happy times.

When I was a child we would play games – dominoes, Happy Families and things like that. I'm sure you are probably thinking that all my memories have a rosy glow, but this is really how it was. And these games can be quite intense, you know, even Happy Families! The person asking you if you've got a particular card would sometimes spin out their request with a long preamble before they would say which card they were after – prolonging the agony. How we used to dread, as children, being asked for a card that we had got, and having to part with it. How triumphant we would feel when we could say, 'Not at home', and then it was our turn. My grandmother, if she was losing at dominoes, made you change seats. She would say, 'You're in the lucky seat! I'll sit there!' and we all had to change round.

It all sounds like something and nothing, but happiness seems to come from ordinary things.

After I was married, we were able to spend a lot of time together when the girls were growing up, because John's school holidays were the same as theirs. We had a car, and we used to go out for the day to various places. There was a family with children next door, and Katherine spent nearly as much time next door as in her own home, because these children were older and she liked to tag on.

Once we had moved back to Dukinfield, near to the church, we all became very involved with that. Katherine and Susan were attendants to the Rose Queens at Sunday

School, and then they were both Rose Queens in turn themselves. The Rose Queen was the girl with the highest attendance at Sunday School that year. On Saturday nights throughout the summer the Rose Queen and her retinue of all the other children from the Sunday School visited all the different churches in the neighbouring parishes. There was a crowning ceremony too for the Rose Queen, for which she wore a beautiful gown. Katherine and Susan also were always in all the church pantomimes and plays, because we did a lot of amateur dramatics at St Mark's in those days. They went to a convent school in Romiley, and they were both in the choir. So in the evenings we had to take them to and from rehearsals.

That's one of the worst things about being a parent – all the running around you have to do!

Understanding each other's point of view

You can't just lay down the law and say, 'Because I say so …' Everyone sees things differently. However strongly you feel that you know what is best for your children, it is better to say, 'Well, let's talk about it – if you do it this way, this might happen, and if you do it the other way, then that might happen. The decision is yours.'

You hope that they will then see the sense in your way of thinking, and give up their idea if it was a stupid one. It is very frustrating, of course, when you've done all that and they still choose to do the wrong thing. But at least you've given them the benefit of your advice. You have to think, 'Well, it's up to them now.' I don't think you should ever try to direct your children's lives for them.

Mother knows best

I was quite a firm parent, because children often try to 'put up for boss' if you aren't. I think John and I were both quite strict, but never so that the children had any fear. I think if you smack a child, then it makes them more belligerent, and inclined to try to get their own back – either on you or by taking it out on a smaller child. We used to say, 'Don't do that, or you may hurt yourself.' Or, 'Don't do that or there's going to be an accident – you'll knock things over.' If they were really naughty we used to send them up to their bedroom until they decided to say they were sorry. Invariably they'd stay up for five minutes and then they'd come down and say, 'I'm sorry' – although sometimes with a very cross face. And we'd say, 'Right you are. Carry on playing now then.' I think it is very important to talk to your children, rather than shouting at them or giving them a slap.

My own mother was quite firm. If we had something painful like a septic boil, she'd get all the poison out however much you were suffering. 'It's got to come out. It's no good leaving it in there.'

I'd say, 'Ooh! Mother! That hurts. *Please* leave it.' But I suppose with being a nurse, she knew what she had to do, and she took no notice of my pleas. She was really good. Very warm, but very firm.

She said that she learned one lesson from me very early on, because when I was a tiny girl she said to me, 'If you do that again, I shall smack you ...' A few minutes later I came up to her and said, 'You should have smacked me then. I did it again.' She thought, 'Oh dear! Now what do I do?' So she always said that it was me who had taught her that if you threaten something, you've got to carry it through.

One thing my mother used to say, whenever we were undecided about what to do, was, 'Well, sit down and try to think how you would feel if you suddenly couldn't do it.' It was a good idea, a bit like tossing a coin, heads you do it, tails you don't do it, and it comes down tails … then you immediately know that you really do want to do it. So you do it!

When I was leaving home for the first time and going to work in my first professional engagement on the stage as a student-actress in Scotland, I began to get cold feet just before I left. I thought, 'I don't know if I ought to go. It's such a long way.' I had a very good job as a secretary and I was giving it up. My mother said, 'Well, just sit down and think, "How would I feel about it if I suddenly *couldn't* go?"'

So I did this, and when I had sat and thought for a few seconds, I said, 'I'm going!'

When John and I were looking for our first house to buy, and weren't sure how to make up our minds, my mother said, 'Give it points for and against, and then reckon them up.'

This is how she did everything. She didn't ever tell us what to do but she helped us to make our own decisions. She showed us how to focus on things.

Katherine's cheque

Sometimes, however much you think your child should do one thing, they firmly decide to do the opposite. When she left school, our daughter Katherine went to teachers' training college in Manchester. Her best friend, Kathryn Finneran, went to the same college, but when they got to the practical side of the course and started going out into schools for teaching practice, Kathryn decided that she didn't want to go on with it any more. So our Katherine decided that she didn't want to go on with it any more either. They've always been bonded very closely, and still are. So Katherine just left college and came home.

I was annoyed. I said to her, 'Just think of all the things you'll be giving up – a job for life, and working with children which is what you always wanted to do.' I told her to sit down and think what she had given up before it was too late. But she was quite adamant. I don't know why. She always wanted to work with children, but she just threw it away. And yet she has never, ever said since that she thought it had been a mistake to give up teaching. I wondered if it would have happened if she'd gone to a college farther away, or if she'd gone to a different college from Kathryn. You can't help thinking sometimes, 'Life would have been different if … ' But really it's no good thinking that way.

I felt then that she was throwing away her whole future career, and I still think she would have made a wonderful teacher, like her father. I thought, 'Well, right, if she's left college, and left a good career, then until she gets a job, that's it, she gets nothing.' So I said to her, 'You go back to college, or you get yourself a job, otherwise there's no money. You stay at home and do nothing.'

What happened? I'll tell you what happened. Social Security sent her a cheque – she didn't even have to go and sign on. So she could do what she liked. They just took the responsibility away from me. I felt she had to understand what she was giving up, and that my way was the best way of showing her that, but I wasn't allowed to show her this.

When I was young, if you hadn't got work you had to queue all day to sign on and then you had to go back and stand in line again for hours and hours to be given something like ten shillings. It was awful. People who were out of work for a long time developed a permanent 'dole-queue shuffle'. St Paul says, 'He who does not work shall not eat.' I personally think we ought to get back to something like that for those who shun work offered to them.

As it turned out, Katherine soon got bored with having no work, and started training as a dental assistant, working for a Mr Payne who lived in a house he called 'Tooth Acre'. Can you believe it? I couldn't bear to spend my days looking into people's mouths, but Katherine has never said she regretted giving up her plan to be a teacher, and I know that she has thoroughly enjoyed her work in dentistry ever since.

STRATEGIES FOR PLAYING THE GAME

* Learning to share is learning to care.

* Allow a little rain to fall in your life – it will make it bloom.

* Treasure your memories.

* Too much too soon can lead to great harm – keep some pleasures for the future.

* Talk things through – don't lay down the law.

* Respect your children's decisions – even when they go completely against your own very wise advice!

'Better a dry crust with peace and quiet than a house full of feasting, with strife' (*Proverbs 17:1, NIV*).

7
'NOT AT HOME'

After all the cards have been dealt, each Player takes it in turn to ask for the Character Cards that they need to complete their own Happy Families. If you have, for example, Mr Bun the Baker or Miss Bun in your own hand, you can ask for the other members of the Bun family, one at a time, to complete the set. If the Player you ask has got that card, he or she must hand it over to you, and then you can ask another Player for another card. If they've got it, they have to give it to you, but if they haven't, they say, 'Not at Home', and then it's their turn.

For families trying to be happy in the real world, 'Not at Home' can have a sad ring to it.

The decline of the neighbourhood family

When they moved people from neighbourly rows of terrace houses into blocks of high-rise flats, it was the beginning of the break-up of British family life as we knew it. After the war, in an attempt to clean up some of the poorer districts of the big cities, people were moved out of their familiar surroundings. They were moved out from where they knew everybody in the street, out from where they had known one another all their lives, and for generations, out from where everybody helped one another. Then the bulldozers knocked down all the old houses and up went great high-rise flats instead, often on huge estates miles away from the centre of town. Sometimes that took all the younger members of families away and left the old people behind. The architects and planners were only trying to make everyone's lives better, I know, but it was a disaster. High-rises and faraway estates worked against family life, and against neighbourliness. People became prisoners in their high-rise flats, lonely and cut off from everything familiar. They had a lovely view of a world that they couldn't get in touch with. And you needed a head for heights – which my Auntie Florrie didn't have.

When they moved my Uncle Peter and his wife into a high-rise flat in Salford, Auntie Florrie never went out or even looked out again. She didn't even like to go near the windows. They were thirteen storeys up, and she had been used to living in a little house with friends all round, neighbours who you could chat to, and who would help you with whatever you needed. As I've said before, your street was an extension of the family. You knew all your neighbours, and they all used to come in and out of your house, and it was always the same. If you needed anything, you asked your neighbour.

From my autograph book:

Friendships are better than battleships.
Dorothy Ashe, 8.10.43

Playing in the street

How many children do you see playing games outside nowadays? If you see a group of children outside today, you wonder what they are up to. (The way Nora Batty thinks whenever she sees Compo! He must be up to something.) We used to play all sorts of games in the street.

We had seasons for different games. For a while, it would all be skipping ... 'All in together – the cows in the meadow ... When I count twenty – the rope must be empty. Five, ten, fifteen, twenty!' You would get six or eight girls all skipping together inside a big long rope, which was probably their mother's clothes-line, being turned by two others. Or we tied the rope round a lamp-post, the old-fashioned kind with the bars across. You used to swing on this rope round the lamp, and suddenly you'd nearly fly. I used to love swinging round the lamp-post. And then, at another time of year, it would be all ball games. If there were a few of you, one would throw the ball over her head and then turn round and she'd have to guess who had caught it.

There was very little traffic when I was young. Hardly anyone had a car. Nowadays, with the breakdown of the neighbourhood communities, children don't know one another, and their parents daren't allow them to play in the streets like we used to because of the traffic and the dangerous people you read about in the newspapers. So they stay indoors and watch far too much television because there is nothing else to do.

When my girls were young, there used to be a May Queen for May Day, just in our little close, made up of a few houses and bungalows, and either Katherine or Susan or one of the girls from next door would be the May Queen for that year. We'd dress the May Queen up in a veil and long white dress, and the other girls and boys would dress up as nursery rhyme characters – Georgie Porgy, Little Tommy Tucker. The old folk really loved to watch them parade around the close, especially when one of the children played the recorder as they went along.

Helping your children to manage change

Happiness can be a matter of luck – you can't altogether control it. Stability is an ingredient of a happy family life, but it can't always be arranged. Then you have to find ways to make up for it.

I realise that other people have many more difficulties and problems than we had. We had stability. John was teaching at a school, so our family life had to be based nearby. He was nearly twenty-five years at his last school, all the time that the children were growing up. I might have had to travel away for my work sometimes, but their base was always secure at our home near where John was working.

Families who have to move from place to place because of their work have a very difficult time of it. The children are taken away from one school, and have to start again in a new school where everyone else has already formed friendships before they arrive, so often they get bullied. And they can't find people to play with at home either, because they don't know the other children in their road or block of flats. Children are often quite shy, and established groups of friends don't like outsiders coming in. So it's very unsettling for them. They need a lot of extra help to cope with all these changes – you can't expect them to sort it out by themselves.

That's why I can't say too often how important I think the local church is in the life of a young family. Wherever you move to, there will be a church with people who can introduce you to the community around your new home. At the very least it will be a great source of information about what is going on. There will be Mother and Toddler groups, Youth Clubs and societies that different members of the family might want to join. There will be other people with children whom your own children can meet and get to know. If there's an elderly relative as part of your family circle, the church will often have a Luncheon Club once a week for senior citizens in the area.

The family is at the heart of all Christian life, beginning with a homeless family in Bethlehem.

The centre of life

The church was always the centre.

The church and the vicarage were always built in the centre of the village or town, and the annual church fetes used to take place in the vicarage garden, and all round the church. Most of the churches are still there, still at the heart of the community, but many of the old vicarages are not.

I think they have made a mistake selling off so many of the old vicarages, and building small, modern ones. I know the vicar's family may be young and modern and not want to live in an old Victorian building, but I still think it's sad. You can't go and knock on the door next to the church any more and expect to find your vicar. You will probably find a commuting businessman and his family live there now – and they're out. The vicarages have been bought and turned into private homes by the well-to-do, or even turned into private hotels and Bed and Breakfast establishments. The modern vicarage can be some distance from the church.

I think it's a shame, and I think they should have modernised the old vicarages. They were where we still need them, next to the church. If they are too big for a modern family, they could have part of it, and turn the extra space into consulting rooms for the church offices and for other professional people, like the local doctor or dentist or undertaker. Many of the old vicarages, standing in the middle of the community, were sold for a song, although nowadays they fetch huge prices. Meanwhile the new house was bought at great expense, and it hasn't been of any value to the church family for the vicar to be 'Not at Home'.

The family doctor

Another person who is 'Not at Home' any more is the doctor. They used to be part of the family, and often delivered several generations of the same family. Our Dr Gordon lived on King Street. In the big house opposite to us lived Dr Bryce and his daughter, who became the first female doctor in the area, Dr Gladys Bryce, but they weren't our doctors. Our doctor was Dr Gordon, on King Street, near the Town Hall. He would come at any time day or night, whenever he was needed he would be there. He was often also a wise counsellor and friend.

Of course, it wasn't free. People couldn't just go to the doctor like they do now. My mother used to put money aside every week for the doctor's bill, so when any of the family were ill there was money there to pay the doctor. Nowadays some people go to the doctor for every little thing. And even for the big things – there's so much more you can have done now – and it's all free.

Doctors today may not be part of the family in the same way, and they may not always remember our names, but we need to treasure them and respect them just as much as we did in the old days. Doctors today work under very great pressure. They have to see many, many more patients than in the old days, with several thousand patients on their books and more than they can be expected to remember by name. But we should remember them in our prayers, because they try very hard to help keep our families well and happy, and that is why they are sometimes 'Not at Home' themselves.

The cost of living

When both parents are forced to work full time, some children come home from school and there's *nobody* at home. Or the parents work shifts, so as one comes in, the other goes out. They've got to – the price of things now is unbelievable, isn't it? I don't know how young people ever manage to amass enough money to put a deposit on a house in the first place, let alone keep up the payments on the mortgage.

The first house we bought was brand-new, semi-detached, three bedrooms, and with a front and back garden. It cost us £1,550. What could you get for that now? I know wages weren't as high then ... but even so. The smallest house today – what is it? You can't get much anywhere under £35,000 today. You often have to pay £5,000 just for a garage. I feel for those young couples who both have to go out to work in order to make enough money to pay the mortgage.

When I started working, if you were prepared to work there was work available. But now, young people finish at university and they can't get a job. It must be so worrying for them. And people who have worked hard and thought they were in jobs for life, workers in big factories, businesspeople, professional people, teachers, television producers – anyone can be made redundant today. It really is frightening. It must be soul destroying after working really hard, suddenly to be pushed out and unemployed. I think we are all put under far too much pressure now. How can home life be anything but anxious and stressful? And what effect is that having on our children?

I'm sorry if I'm being rather controversial, but there's another thing I'd change if I were the Prime Minister. The government now pays money so that women can go back to work as soon as they've had their babies, and to pay to have them looked after by someone else. I think that is all wrong. I think the government should pay for the mothers to stay at home, not for them to go out to work. It's only four and a half years before the children start school. It's not a long time to spend 'at home' with your own children, is it?

Working mother

I left work as soon as I knew I was pregnant. I was fortunate, because John was a teacher. Even though it was a small wage compared with these days, it was enough for us to live on. We learned how to cut a small meat pie into four parts. I never intended to go back to work until both children were at school, and then only during the day. Oldham Rep said I could always work for them at any time, but it was evening work, and I would have been going out every day just as the children were coming in. I never wanted that; I always wanted to look after them, put them to bed, and get them up in the morning.

It was only when Gerald Harper phoned me and said, 'Why aren't you working in television now Granada has started in Manchester?' that things started to change. When I told him about the children, he said, 'Oh, you could still do television work and look after your children. You work during the day. When they come home from school, you'll be there.'

In fact, Susan hadn't yet started school when I started doing 'extra' work, but I wouldn't really call myself a working mother. I never needed to leave them for any length of time, and when I did, it was their grandma (my mother) or John who collected them from school, people they loved. Nowadays, without the extended family and with so many single-parent families, there's often nobody there to help a young mother.

I was not away a lot. I was lucky if I got one day's work in a month. Two days was exceptionally lucky. Sometimes I'd go for months without getting anything at all. In *Coronation Street* if you had a walk-on part, you'd either get one or two days' work. It was wonderful if you got two days – but then it would be at least another month before anything else came along. By jingo, we'd have been in the money if I'd got work every day. I got £3 a day for extra work. I used to put any money I earned to one side, and we used it for our holidays.

Not many of us have little budget jars any more, do we? One jar for the rent man, one for the gas, one for the electric, and one for the holiday? We did that for years.

Make yourself at home

Another secret of happy family life is all working together to make your home a nice place to live. If a house is a pigsty, if every room is full of dirt and mess, nobody is going to want to spend much time there. What is the good of schools teaching children about 'tidy-up time' at the end of each day when their mother and father never tidy up at home? You should all treasure your home. However small a place it is, and even if you are only renting it, as long as your family lives there, it is 'home'.

Home alone

There's only John and me here now. Our chicks have flown the nest, but we see as much of them as we can. Our daughters are both very independent girls. As I have already mentioned, Susan has become a vicar in the Church of England so her home at the moment is her vicarage in the south of England. Of course we go to see her, and she comes to see us, but naturally we see more of Katherine, who lives nearby. But neither of them would want to share a home with us again. It's different when they are children, and you are in charge, but once they've been running their own lives and their own home, I don't think they ever want to go back to living in their parent's home. You never think of your children as getting older, really, do you? They are always your 'children'.

We nearly always see Katherine in the week for a meal, and we all sing in the choir on Sunday at church, and very often she comes home with us for a proper family Sunday lunch (with a pudding!) afterwards. Sometimes when she comes round we will sit and watch television together. Sunday is my favourite evening for television, because we watch *Last of the Summer Wine*, which is our kind of humour, and *Songs of Praise*, which as Christians we all like, especially now we have the words on the screen. Then there is *The Antiques Road Show*, when we all try to guess how much the things are going to be worth. We really enjoy that. So Sunday night for us is a good one. We're simple folk with simple pleasures you see!

When your children grow up and leave home – and it happens so fast you can hardly believe it – you realise how lucky you were to have had them. Make the most of all your family members while they are still 'at home'. Don't take happiness for granted.

> *To be happy at home is the ultimate result of all ambition, the end to which every enterprise and labour tends, and of which every desire prompts the prosecution.*
>
> Samuel Johnson, *The Rambler*

STRATEGIES FOR COPING WHEN PEOPLE ARE 'NOT AT HOME'

* Get to know your neighbours and your neighbours' children.

* Show your children how to make a communal skipping rope.

* Remember that your children will need lots of extra help when you move house.

* Use your local church to find out what is going on in your area, and join in.

* Don't take happiness for granted.

* Keep the home fires burning.

And Ruth said, 'Entreat me not to leave thee, or to return from following after thee: for whither thou goest, I will go; and where thou lodgest, I will lodge: thy people shall be my people, and thy God my God' *(Ruth 1:16, AV)*.

8:
THE OPTIONAL 'PLEASE' AND 'THANK YOU' RULE

When you play Happy Families, the 'Please' and 'Thank You' rule is optional. I would have thought it should be compulsory!

It is obviously a rule that is treated as optional by the television companies these days. Very few plays and series, even when they are supposed to be comedies, are about families who ever say 'Please' or 'Thank You', or who are even barely civil to each other. If television producers are depicting family life as they think it really is, then I can only say, 'Thank goodness I don't know many families like theirs!'

Uncle Fred's strategy

If someone calls to see you, whether it's for business or pleasure, the first thing that should be turned off is the television, however interesting the programme you are watching. You can't talk properly with that box blaring away in the background. Your friends deserve more of your attention than that. And these days, if you've got a video recorder, you've really no excuse.

In the early days of television, if my Uncle Fred called on friends and they didn't turn off their set while he was there, what he would do when he got home was to telephone them and say, 'Now tell me, how are you?'

They would usually say, 'Well, you've only just left!'

'Yes, but I didn't get to know how you were, and have a proper chat, because you didn't switch off the television.'

Nora Batty sounds off

Nora Batty has been a wonderful character to play over the years, with her rage, her goodness and her obsessive cleanliness. Her sudden feelings of tenderness for Compo – when she thinks he's ill or in danger. And you can be sure, Nora doesn't have much time to sit and watch her black-and-white television set. She would be outraged if she did, and would probably brush it out of her front door with her broom, sending it hurtling down the steps. She would definitely be 'Not at Home' to Mr Rude.

It's been such a happy show, *Last of the Summer Wine*, where the sexiest things are Nora's wrinkled stockings and Marina waddling around in her tight mini-skirt. So many people thank me – although it's got nothing to do with me, really – for all the pleasure it gives, and they say, 'It's one of the few shows left where we can all sit down together and watch it as a family.'

Nora Batty is a larger than life character, which is probably why I'm so often asked to play the Dame in pantomime. In fact, *Last of the Summer Wine* itself is like a kind of pantomime. The three men certainly haven't grown up. They are three Peter Pans, still doing pranks and still up to the things they must have got up to when they were naughty boys. No wonder the women lose patience. But the relationship between Nora and Compo was a beautiful thing. People were always asking me when Nora and Compo were going to marry. I used to think it could only happen in the very last episode ever – but now it will never be.

Everyone behaving badly

Television should be setting a high moral standard, not reflecting a collapse in morality. For most of us, surely, life is far more harmonious than as we see it so often portrayed on the screens? I can't believe in a family where one son is on drugs, one daughter is an alcoholic, and another has murdered her auntie – and all in one single family.

With some of the programmes that have been shown recently, I honestly believe television writers are just seeing how far they can go before there is a public outcry to put a stop to it. I think some scenes are put in purely for shock value, and have nothing to do with good drama or good comedy.

There is supposed to be a watershed at 9 o'clock, before

which it is safe for the whole family to watch together. But you only need to watch an episode of *Emmerdale*, *Coronation Street* or *EastEnders*, all well before the watershed, to see enough sex, drugs and violence to make you wonder what on earth the world is coming to. It's giving such a terrible picture of life, and life is not like that for most of us. If you have God in your life, it cannot be like that.

Comedy has to be believable. There have always been comedies that show the funny side of life as it really is. Among my favourites are *Dad's Army*, *The Good Life*, and *To the Manor Born*, and recently one of our great favourites, *As Time Goes By*. I'd have liked to have been in that – I would have made them an excellent housekeeper! Sid Lotterby tells me they may be doing another series soon, and I do hope so. John and I both love it.

Television can bring strangers and unwelcome guests into our homes. It can also be the window through which we meet old friends, and some can become almost like family. But we are definitely 'Not at Home' to the revolting Mr Rude.

TV dinners

With so many of the things you see on television giving such a distorted picture of family life, I don't think it's a good idea to leave the education and entertainment of our children up to the television when they are at home. In some ways the medium of television is a blessing, but in other ways it isn't. It's a blessing for old people, and if you're ill or on your own. But the younger generation should be doing other things.

So many children come home and sit and watch television even while they are eating their meals. Sitting in front of the television with a burger or pizza in their hand, watching people behaving badly, isn't going to teach them anything much at all, least of all about how to live a happy family life.

More recently, it isn't only the television they watch all day, with cartoons showing day and night – it's also their computers. Many children seem to be just as addicted to computers as they previously were to television. Parents used to have to drag their children away from sitting in front of the television screens, now it is from sitting too long in front of their computers.

Television is like blotting paper for the mind if it doesn't stimulate the imagination. At least some of the computer games are educational and interactive – children aren't just sitting there passively watching. I suppose many youngsters are learning something from their computers, and it would be hard to use the computer and eat a burger at the same time! But too much time spent sitting indoors staring at any kind of screen will make them edgy and cross. They need to go outside and play. There's so much they're missing in the real world if they spend too much time indoors.

The lost art of conversation

A family meal is everyone sitting round the table, eating with a knife and fork, and talking to each other. You can hardly get a word out of some children nowadays, even older ones. If they never sit down together with their parents and brothers and sisters round the meal table and have a conversation, how will they learn how to behave when they go out for a meal with colleagues at work, or a boyfriend or girlfriend later in life? Lots of them start primary school without even having been taught how to hold a knife and fork

I don't mean that you should be discussing world peace with your four-year-old. Discuss the day's events. What did Miss King say about his sums, and who won the neatness prize for handwriting at school? Did anyone get into trouble for anything? Do they want to bring a friend home for tea? What homework have they got?

You can tell them about the cat being sick, or the hamster nearly escaping. Or vice versa. I don't know – there's a million things to talk about once you get into the way of it. If children don't learn how to make conversation and have good manners when they are at home with their family, I don't see how they will ever learn.

Saying Grace – God's 'Please' and 'Thank you' rule

When we were children, we would all sit round the tea table and at the beginning my mother would say Grace. At the end we were taught to say, 'Thank you, God, for a lovely meal. Please may I leave the table?' After every meal we always had to say that before we were allowed to leave the table, and I brought my children up to do the same. After tea they were allowed to watch children's television, but only for an hour. After that we used to turn it off and say, 'That's enough.' On a nice evening, they would go outside and play.

I'm afraid that John and I don't say Grace now that there are just the two of us at the kitchen table. We should do, but we don't. And we don't ask one another for permission to get down from the table either! But we do sit at table together, and talk to each other, and I hope we remember to be sincerely thankful.

Selkirk Grace

Some have meat but canna' eat,
Some could eat, but want it,
But I ha' meat, and I can eat,
And may the Lord be thankit

STRATEGIES FOR THE 'PLEASE' AND 'THANK YOU' RULE

* Turn off the television when visitors arrive.

* Don't believe the picture of family life that's shown on television soap operas.

* Don't leave all the education and entertainment of your family up to the television set and computer games.

* Share one family meal a day, when everyone sits round the table and talks.

* Help bring back the lost art of conversation.

* Remember God's 'Please' and 'Thank You' rule.

And he took bread, gave thanks and broke it, and gave it to them, saying, 'This is my body given for you; do this in remembrance of me' (*Luke 22:19, NIV*).

9
THE WINNER

The Winner takes all. In the game, the Winner is the one who has collected the most 'Happy Families' and laid them down on the table. He or she then scoops up all the counters in the Counters Pool.

The family that wins happiness in life is one where children know they are loved, and parents know that they have given everything they are able to give to enable their children to grow up to be free and happy individuals. The winner is love.

The first Christian family

God loved the world, and when he wanted to save it from a downward spiral of misery and sin, he didn't send a giant or an army, he sent his son.

Jesus was born into a human family that was very poor. He was there in the manger with all the animals. He could hardly have been born into worse circumstances when you think about it. He couldn't have had a more lowly start in life, and yet this is what God arranged. There were no televisions, no radios, and certainly no internet in those days and yet since the birth in Bethlehem of this little baby, Jesus' teaching about love has spread throughout the whole world, and kings and queens, rulers and princes, have worshipped him.

Teach me to live

The church choir at St Mark's at one time consisted almost entirely of our family members. As I mentioned in Chapter 1, there were sixteen of us at the height: my cousins, Frances and Janet; Janet's husband, Cyril, who was the organist, and their daughters, Stella and Lucy; Lucy's husband, Ian, and Sarah, their daughter; my Cousin Leonard's two daughters, Carolyn and Joanne; Carolyn's husband, Ian; Uncle Sam; Uncle Harry; and, last but not least, John, Katherine, Susan and me. That is the most there ever was at one time, but we didn't stop there.

Today in the choir we also have Lisa, who is Frances' granddaughter, and Richard, her grandson, who is a server. But of course they are much younger than the rest of us and weren't there with all the others, so it would be cheating to count them in to make it eighteen family members in the same choir!

My Uncle Sam always sang the bass solo. He had a wonderful voice. I just wished we'd recorded him, along with my mother's beautiful soprano. But there you are, we didn't have good tape recorders in those days. It wasn't as easy then as it would be now.

Once when I was a guest on the *Russell Harty Show*, the whole choir were invited to be in the audience, along with Dennis Thomas, our vicar, and we closed the show by singing our special St Mark's hymn, 'Teach me to live'. It was written over one hundred years ago. We always sing that hymn at St Mark's on special occasions. John and I had it at our wedding. I think these words pretty well sum up the Staff family philosophy:

> *Teach me to live, for life before me lies*
> *An unknown path to yonder Paradise;*
> *Dangers abound and round me, Lord, I see*
> *Are other paths that lead away from Thee.*

> *Teach me to live; with sunny words of cheer,*
> *To brighten life and dry a brother's tear;*
> *Songs for the sad, a lift for heavy load,*
> *A heart to win a wanderer back to God.*

Remembering

My mother always believed that when Jesus broke the bread and said, 'Do this in memory of me' he meant that every time you had a meal you should remember him. She thought that he was always there, in the middle of our everyday lives. That didn't mean just when you drank the wine and ate the bread in church at communion. She said that if she were on a desert island she would still remember Christ every time she ate or drank. This is what she believed he meant. Whether this is right or not, I don't know, but my mother strongly believed it.

From my autograph book:

Here is another small selection of some of the wit and wisdom of the Higginbottoms. I've grown quite used to signing other people's autograph books these days, but I had two or three little collections of my own when I was a young girl. When I was young, I didn't seem to have met anyone famous to get an autograph, I just seem to have done the rounds of my own family:

> *Do all the good you can to all the people you can in all the places you can whenever you can.*
>
> Mother

> *When up to your neck in hot water, be like the kettle and sing!*
>
> Dad

> *When your luck is out, put 'p' before it.*
>
> Dear old Uncle Sam

> *The future lies before you like a sheet of driven snow*
> *Be careful how you choose your steps, for every step will show.*
>
> Auntie Alice Gregson

> *Don't just look at your hill – climb it.*
>
> Connie, my sister

Whoever you are, be noble,
Whatever you do, do well,
Whenever you speak, speak kindly
Give joy wherever you dwell.

That's in my mother's handwriting. Well, I've tried!

Saying your prayers

When they were children, Susan and Katherine always said their prayers at night, kneeling by the bed. I don't think they had problems about religion. If they ever had any questions, they must have received the right answers.

When they were small, they went to Sunday School, so they knew all about Jesus. Later they went to a convent school. We chose it purely because it was the best school in the area, and when they went we realised why it was the best – because everything was based on respect for the nuns. You never saw children behaving badly. The nuns just used to glance – and that was enough. I never ever heard the nuns raise their voices. I've never seen a school with pupils so well behaved. All the children respected the nuns.

We have always prayed together at home as a family. We believe our prayers are heard. When someone we know has been ill we have gathered together and prayed for them and their family. When we are discussing someone who is seriously ill, Susan might say, 'Shall we all pray together?' We usually hold hands, just sitting together in the sitting-room. You don't need to kneel down to say prayers. You can say them wherever you are. Susan usually starts off, and we all try to say something. Yes. We do pray.

I talked in an earlier chapter about house groups. I've just heard of one village in Kent that wanted to have an ecumenical prayer group, meeting in one another's homes. But at the beginning everyone felt too embarrassed to speak up. It can feel awkward to start to pray in what looks like a normal social gathering, especially when you aren't used to it. One of the Catholic members of the group suggested that they all put paper bags over their heads, so they couldn't see one another! They did it too, all of them, even the local MP's wife, and it worked. Now the group meets regularly, Catholics, Church of England, Methodists and searchers, and they don't need paper bags any more!

Families that pray together stay together

For my family our Christian faith has made all the difference in the world. Belief in God is something you take with you wherever you go. Even when everything seems lost, when you are far from home, if you believe in God you have something to live for. It is the one thing that even the worst misfortune and unhappy circumstances cannot take from you. It is always there, something to base your hope for the future on.

My mother's and my father's family both attended St Mark's Church, Dukinfield, which is how they met. Members of the two families are still together all these years on and there are about a dozen of us living around about who attend St Mark's regularly and pray together. Some branches of the family have moved away, of course, but even so we are still in communication.

My cousin, Leonard Bainbridge, went to work in Australia about twenty-five years ago, and now lives in New Zealand. (He was named after my Uncle Leonard, of course, who was killed in the First World War.) When he came over to the UK last Christmas for a holiday, he first of all turned up to see me in *Aladdin*, and then he gave the whole family, all sixty of us (yes, we are sixty!), a great big party because he'd come home.

Millennium Christmas

For years, every Christmas, our choir would sing Stainer's *Crucifixion*.

> God so loved the world
> That He gave His only begotten Son
> To the end that whoso believeth in Him
> Should not perish, but have everlasting life.
> God sent not his Son into the world
> To condemn the world
> But that the world
> Through Him might be saved ...

You can't paint it. You can't describe it with words. But the offer is there. You either believe in the love of God or you don't. I do believe, and whenever we sang those words to the beautiful music in *The Crucifixion*, I used to be almost in tears.

Most families try to be together at Christmas. Even those who forget about Christianity for the rest of the year seem to feel moved by the Christmas story. There's an atmosphere in church on Christmas night and Christmas morning, quite different from at any other time. It's not just the candlelight and the crib and the carols. The whole town seems to suspend all doubts and criticisms of church and religion for a while, and comes together as a community. The church congregations expand, not only with the addition of the family's children and grandchildren home for the holiday, but with people from the town who never come at any other time. I wish we could somehow harness that beautiful, joyful spirit, and make it happen more often.

One way to help that, I'm convinced, is if families came together more often, not once a year, not only at Christmas, but as much as possible. Even if it's only making a regular telephone call. Spending time together, keeping in contact, is one of the great secrets of a happy family life. Being there.

At the end of next year it will be 2,000 years since the first Christmas. What better gift can we offer a baby born in a stable in Bethlehem than a loving welcome in our own families? What better way of celebrating the 2,000th Christmas than by making our communities places where the spirit of Christmas is at work all the year round?

STRATEGIES FOR THE WINNER

* Let your children know that they are loved.

* Remember how loved you are.

* Have faith in God.

* When you are up to your neck in hot water –
  think of the kettle and sing!

* Have family gatherings more than once a
  year, and keep in touch by letter and
  telephone.

* Love one another.

'He that loveth not knoweth not God; for God is love' (1 John 4:8, AV).

ENDGAME

There is no endgame. The truth is I want to end this book with my favourite prayer – which is the beautiful Psalm 121 – 'I will lift up mine eyes unto the hills'. I can't think of a better way to end this little collection of thoughts. I hope you feel, like me, that we must never give up trying to keep family life going through the new millennium, because of the happiness it brings.

I was born and grew up beside great hills. I sometimes feel my life would go flat if I lived somewhere flat.

My hills are the Pennines, which go right down the centre of the country. At school we were taught it was the backbone of England. I draw great comfort and strength from the Pennines. I know that was how my father felt too, after the war, when he was a storeman, and would stand at the open door of the mill, looking across the valley to the hills beyond.

I can recite Psalm 121 by heart, and have written it here from memory – but you will have to take my word for it!

PSALM 121

I will lift up mine eyes unto the hills, from whence cometh my help.

My help cometh even from the Lord, who hath made heaven and earth.

He will not suffer thy foot to be moved: and he that keepeth thee will not sleep.

Behold, he that keepeth Israel shall neither slumber nor sleep.

The Lord himself is thy keeper: the Lord is thy defence upon thy right hand.

So that the sun shall not burn thee by day, neither the moon by night.

The Lord shall preserve thee from all evil: yea, it is even he that shall keep thy soul.

The Lord shall preserve thy going out and thy coming in from this time forth, for evermore. Amen.

KATHY STAFF

MY STORY – WRINKLES AND ALL

*'Minnie / Nora / Kathy by any name is a force
no mortal can resist.'*

The *Daily Mail*

Kathy Staff's part as Nora Batty in *Last of the Summer Wine* has made her a household name. This autobiography celebrates *Last of the Summer Wine* which, in its 27th year, is television's longest running comedy. It also reveals the fascinating life and faith of Britain's most unlikely sex symbol.

Christened Minnie Higginbottom, Kathy started her career in 1949 with weekly repertory companies but, after marriage to John and the birth of two daughters, decided to concentrate on television. She went on to play several roles in *Coronation Street* and in *Crossroads*, making her one of the most popular characters in TV soap opera. She has played numerous theatre roles and has delighted audiences with her many appearances in panto. Beneath the larger than life characters she so often portrays, is a thoughtful and deeply spiritual person, very active and involved in her local church.

Hodder & Stoughton
0 340 69470 X